HAY FEVER

by
NOËL COWARD

SAMUEL FRENCH

LONDON

NEW YORK TORONTO SYDNEY HOLLYWOOD

ISBN 0 573 01174 5

Please see page iv for further copyright information.

HAY FEVER

Produced at the Ambassadors Theatre, London, on 8th June, 1925, with the following cast of characters—

JUDITH BLISS	*Miss Marie Tempest*
DAVID BLISS	*Mr W. Graham Browne*
SOREL BLISS	*Miss Helen Spencer*
SIMON BLISS	*Mr Robert Andrews*
MYRA ARUNDEL	*Miss Hilda Moore*
RICHARD GREATHAM	*Mr Athole Stewart*
JACKIE CORYTON	*Miss Ann Trevor*
SANDY TYRELL	*Mr Patrick Susands*
CLARA	*Miss Minnie Rayner*

The action of the play takes place in the Hall of the Blisses' House at Cookham in June

ACT I
Saturday afternoon

ACT II
Saturday evening

ACT III
Sunday morning

HAY FEVER

ACT I

SCENE—*The Hall of David Bliss's house is very comfortable and extremely untidy.*

There are several of Simon's cartoons scattered about the walls, masses of highly-coloured American and classical music strewn about the piano, and comfortable furniture. A staircase ascends to a small balcony leading to the bedrooms, David's study and Simon's room. There is a door leading to the library down L, *and a service door above it under the stairs. There are french windows at back and the front door on the* R.

(See the Ground Plan at the end of the play)

When the CURTAIN *rises it is about 3 o'clock on a Saturday afternoon in June.* SIMON, *in an extremely dirty tennis shirt and baggy grey flannel trousers, is kneeling in the middle of the floor, drawing on cartridge paper, of which there are two pieces by him.* SOREL, *more neatly dressed, is stretched on the* L *end of the sofa, reading a very violently-bound volume of poems which have been sent to her by an aspiring friend.*

SOREL. Listen to this, Simon. (*She reads*)

> "Love's a Trollop stained with wine,
> Clawing at the breasts of Adolescence,
> Nuzzling, tearing, shrieking, beating—
> God, why were we fashioned so!" (*She laughs*)

SIMON (*looking up from his drawing*) The poor girl's potty!

SOREL. I wish she hadn't sent me the beastly book. I must say something nice about it.

SIMON. The binding's very dashing.

SOREL. She used to be such fun before she married that gloomy little man.

SIMON. She was always a fierce poseuse. It's so silly of people to try and cultivate the artistic temperament. *Au fond* she's just a normal, bouncing Englishwoman.

SOREL. You didn't shave this morning.

SIMON. I know I didn't, but I'm going to in a minute, when I've finished this. (*Pointing to the drawing*)

SOREL. I sometimes wish we were more normal and bouncing, Simon.

SIMON. Why? (*He starts to draw again*)

SOREL. I should like to be a fresh, open-air girl with a passion for games.

Sɪᴍᴏɴ. Thank God you're not.

Sᴏʀᴇʟ. It would be so soothing.

Sɪᴍᴏɴ. Not in this house.

Sᴏʀᴇʟ. Where's Mother?

Sɪᴍᴏɴ. In the garden, practising.

Sᴏʀᴇʟ. Practising?

Sɪᴍᴏɴ (*stopping drawing and looking at Sorel*) She's learning the names of the flowers by heart.

Sᴏʀᴇʟ. What's she up to?

Sɪᴍᴏɴ. I don't know. (*He looks down at the drawing*) Damn! That's crooked.

Sᴏʀᴇʟ. I *always* distrust her when she becomes the Squire's lady.

Sɪᴍᴏɴ. So do I. (*He starts drawing again*)

Sᴏʀᴇʟ. She's been at it hard all day—she tapped the barometer this morning.

Sɪᴍᴏɴ. She's probably got a plan about impressing somebody.

Sᴏʀᴇʟ (*taking a cigarette from the table behind the sofa*) I wonder who.

Sɪᴍᴏɴ. Some dreary, infatuated young man will appear soon, I expect.

Sᴏʀᴇʟ. Not today? (*He lights a cigarette*) You don't think she's asked anyone down today, do you?

Sɪᴍᴏɴ (*stopping drawing and looking up*) I don't know. Has Father noticed anything?

Sᴏʀᴇʟ. No; he's too immersed in work.

Sɪᴍᴏɴ. Perhaps Clara will know.

Sᴏʀᴇʟ. Yell for her.

Sɪᴍᴏɴ (*rising and going up* ᴄ, *calling off at the door below the stairs*) Clara! Clara! . . .

Sᴏʀᴇʟ (*moving to the* ʀ *end of the sofa*) Oh, Simon, I *do* hope she hasn't asked anyone down today.

Sɪᴍᴏɴ (*coming down to the* ʀ *end of the sofa*) Why? Have you?

Sᴏʀᴇʟ. Yes.

Sɪᴍᴏɴ (*crossly*) Why on earth didn't you tell me?

Sᴏʀᴇʟ. I didn't think you'd care one way or another.

Sɪᴍᴏɴ. Who is it?

Sᴏʀᴇʟ. Richard Greatham.

Sɪᴍᴏɴ (*going back to the drawing*) How exciting! I've never heard of him.

Sᴏʀᴇʟ. I shouldn't flaunt your ignorance if I were you—it makes you look silly.

Sɪᴍᴏɴ (*rising and picking up one sheet of cartridge paper, and a pencil*) Well, that's done. (*He rolls up the cartridge paper*)

Sᴏʀᴇʟ. Everybody's heard of Richard Greatham.

Sɪᴍᴏɴ (*amiably*) How lovely for them! (*He goes to the piano*)

Sᴏʀᴇʟ. He's a frightfully well-known diplomatist—I met him at the Mainwarings' dance.

SIMON. He'll need all his diplomacy here. (*He puts the pencil on the piano*)

SOREL. I warned him not to expect good manners, but I hope you'll be as pleasant to him as you can.

SIMON (*moving to* C; *gently*) I've never met any diplomatists, Sorel, but as a class I'm extremely prejudiced against them. They're so suave and polished and debonair.

SOREL. You could be a little more polished without losing caste.

SIMON (*moving to Sorel*) Will he have the papers with him?

SOREL. What papers?

SIMON (*vaguely*) Oh, any papers. (*He goes up* C *and puts the paper on the chair*)

SOREL. I wish you'd confine your biting irony to your caricatures, Simon.

SIMON (*coming down to Sorel*) And I wish you'd confine your girlish infatuations to London, and not force them on your defenceless family.

SOREL. I shall keep him out of your way as much as possible.

SIMON. Do, darling. (*He goes to the piano and lights a cigarette*)

(CLARA *enters from the door below the stairs. She is a hot, round, untidy little woman. She stands* L *by the door*)

(*He sits on the form by the piano*) Clara, has Mother asked anyone down this week-end?

CLARA. I don't know, dear. There isn't much food in the house, and Amy's got toothache.

SOREL. I've got some oil of cloves somewhere.

CLARA. She tried that, but it only burnt her tongue. The poor girl's been writhing about in the scullery like one o'clock.

SOREL. You haven't forgotten to put those flowers in the Japanese room?

SIMON. The Japanese room is essentially feminine, and entirely unsuited to the Pet of the Foreign Office.

SOREL. Shut up, Simon!

CLARA. The room looks lovely, dear—you needn't worry. Just like your mother's dressing-room on a first night.

SIMON. How restful!

CLARA (*moving to Sorel*) Have you told her about your boy friend?

SOREL (*pained*) Not boy friend, Clara.

CLARA (*picking up the drawing that Simon has left on the floor* C) Oh, well, whatever he is. (*she puts the drawing on the chair up* C)

SIMON. I think Sorel's beginning to be ashamed of us all, Clara —I don't altogether blame her; we are very slapdash.

CLARA (*coming down* C; *speaking to Simon*) Are you going to leave that picture in the guests' bathroom, dear? I don't know if it's quite the thing—lots of pink, naked women rolling about in a field.

SIMON (*severely*) Nudity can be very beautiful, Clara.

CLARA. Oh, can it! Perhaps being a dresser for so long 'as spoilt me eye for it.

(CLARA *goes out through the door below the stairs*)

SIMON. Clara's looking tired. We ought to have more servants and not depend on her so much.

SOREL. You know we can never keep them. You're right about us being slapdash, Simon. I wish we weren't.

SIMON. Does it matter?

SOREL. It must, I think—to other people.

SIMON. It's not our fault—it's the way we've been brought up.

SOREL. Well, if we're clever enough to realize that, we ought to be clever enough to change ourselves.

SIMON. I'm not sure that I want to.

SOREL. We're so awfully bad-mannered.

SIMON. Not to people we like.

SOREL. The people we like put up with it because they like *us*.

SIMON. What do you mean, exactly, by bad manners? Lack of social tricks and small-talk?

SOREL. We never attempt to look after people when they come here.

SIMON. Why should we? It's loathsome being looked after.

SOREL. Yes, but people like little attentions. We've never once asked anyone if they've slept well.

SIMON. I consider *that* an impertinence, anyhow.

SOREL. I'm going to try to improve.

SIMON (*putting his feet upon the form*) You're only going on like this because you've got a mania for a diplomatist. You'll soon return to normal.

SOREL (*earnestly*) Abnormal, Simon—that's what we are. Abnormal. People stare in astonishment when we say what we consider perfectly ordinary things. I just remarked at Freda's lunch the other day how nice it would be if someone invented something to make all our faces go up like the Chinese, because I was so bored with them going down. And they all thought I was mad!

SIMON. It's no use worrying, darling; we see things differently, I suppose, and if people don't like it they must lump it.

(JUDITH *enters from the garden. She is carrying an armful of flowers and wearing a tea-gown, a large garden hat, gauntlet gloves and goloshes*)

JUDITH (*coming down to behind the sofa table*) You look awfully dirty, Simon. What have you been doing?

SIMON (*nonchalantly*) Not washing very much.

JUDITH (*putting the basket on the table, and starting to take off her gloves*) You should, darling, really. It's so bad for your skin to leave things about on it.

SOREL. Clara says Amy's got toothache.

JUDITH. Poor dear! There's some oil of cloves in my medicine cupboard. Who is Amy?

SOREL. The scullery-maid, I think.

JUDITH (*putting her gloves on the table and coming* C) How extraordinary! She doesn't look Amy a bit, does she? Much more Flossie. Give me a cigarette.

(SIMON *gives her a cigarette from the box on the piano*)

Delphiniums are those stubby red flowers, aren't they?

SIMON (*lighting a cigarette for Judith*) No, darling; they're tall and blue.

JUDITH. Yes, of course. The red ones are somebody's name— Asters, that's it. I knew it was something opulent. (*She sits on the stool below the piano*)

(SIMON *takes off her goloshes and puts them by the side of the stool*)

I do hope Clara has remembered about the Japanese room.

SOREL. Japanese room!

JUDITH. Yes; I told her to put some flowers in it and take Simon's flannels out of the wardrobe drawer.

SOREL. So did I.

JUDITH (*ominously*) Why?

SOREL (*airily*) I've asked Richard Greatham down for the week-end—I didn't think you'd mind.

JUDITH (*rising and crossing to Sorel*) Mind! How dare you do such a thing?

SOREL. He's a diplomatist.

JUDITH (*going behind the table and starting to sort out the flowers*) That makes it much worse. We must wire and put him off at once.

SOREL. It's too late.

JUDITH. Well, we'll tell Clara to say we've been called away.

SOREL. That would be extremely rude, and, anyhow, I *want* to see him.

JUDITH. You mean to sit there in cold blood and tell me you've asked a complete stranger down for the week-end, and that you *want* to see him!

SOREL. I've often done it before.

JUDITH. I fail to see how that helps matters. Where's he going to sleep?

SOREL. The Japanese room.

JUDITH (*crossing with a bunch of flowers to the table below the door* R) Oh, no, he isn't—Sandy Tyrell is sleeping there.

SIMON (*coming* C) There now! What did I tell you?

SOREL. Sandy—what?

JUDITH. Tyrell, dear.

SIMON. Why didn't you tell us, Mother?

JUDITH (*starting to arrange the flowers in a vase*) I did. I've talked of nothing but Sandy Tyrell for days—I adore Sandy Tyrell.

SIMON (*going back to the form and sitting*) You've never mentioned him.

SOREL. Who is he, Mother?

JUDITH. He's a perfect darling, and madly in love with me— at least, it isn't me really, it's my Celebrated Actress glamour— but it gives me a divinely cosy feeling. I met him at Nora Trent's. (*She crosses to behind the sofa table*)

SOREL. Mother, I wish you'd give up this sort of thing.

JUDITH (*taking more flowers from the basket*) What exactly do you mean by "this sort of thing", Sorel?

SOREL. You know perfectly well what I mean.

JUDITH (*putting down the flowers and going to the R corner of the sofa*) Are you attempting to criticize me?

SOREL. I should have thought you'd be above encouraging silly, callow young men who are infatuated by your name.

JUDITH (*going back to the table and picking up the flowers*) That may be true, but I shall allow nobody but myself to say it. I hoped you'd grow up a good *daughter* to me, not a critical *aunt*.

SOREL (*moving to the L end of the sofa*) It's so terribly cheap.

JUDITH. Cheap! Nonsense! How about your diplomatist?

SOREL. Surely that's a little different, dear?

JUDITH. If you mean that because you happen to be a vigorous *ingénue* of nineteen you have the complete monopoly of any amorous adventure there may be about, I feel it my firm duty to disillusion you.

SOREL. But, Mother——

JUDITH (*crossing to the top end of the piano and picking up the empty vase, which she gives SIMON to hold while she fills it with flowers*) Anyone would think I was eighty, the way you go on. It was a great mistake not sending you to boarding schools, and you coming back and me being your elder sister.

SIMON. It wouldn't have been any use, darling. Everyone knows we're your son and daughter.

JUDITH. Only because I was stupid enough to dandle you about in front of cameras when you were little. I knew I should regret it.

SIMON. I don't see any point in trying to be younger than you are.

JUDITH. At your age, dear, it would be indecent if you did. (*Having finished arranging the flowers, she puts the vase back on the piano, and crosses to the R corner of the sofa*)

SOREL. But, Mother darling, don't you see it's awfully undignified for you to go flaunting about with young men?

JUDITH. I don't flaunt about—I never have. I've been morally

an extremely nice woman all my life—more or less—and if dab-
bling gives me pleasure, I don't see why I *shouldn't* dabble.

SOREL. But it *oughtn't* to give you pleasure any *more*.

JUDITH. You know, Sorel, you grow more damnably feminine
every day. I wish I'd brought you up differently.

SOREL. I'm proud of being feminine.

JUDITH (*sitting on the sofa beside Sorel—kissing her*) You're a
darling, and I adore you; and you're very pretty, and I'm madly
jealous of you.

SOREL (*with her arms round Judith*) Are you really? How lovely!

JUDITH. You will be nice to Sandy, won't you?

SOREL (*sitting up*) Can't he sleep in "Little Hell"?

JUDITH. My dear, he's frightfully athletic and all those hot-
water pipes will sap his vitality.

SOREL. They'll sap Richard's vitality too.

JUDITH. He won't notice them; he's probably used to scorching
tropical Embassies with punkahs waving and everything.

SIMON. He's sure to be deadly, anyhow.

SOREL. You're getting far too blasé and exclusive, Simon.

SIMON. Nothing of the sort. Only I loathe being hearty with
your men friends.

SOREL. You've never been even civil to any of my friends, men
or women.

JUDITH. Don't bicker.

SIMON (*rising and crossing to* c) Anyhow, the Japanese room's a
woman's room, and a woman ought to have it.

JUDITH. I promised it to Sandy—he loves anything Japanese.

SIMON. So does Myra!

JUDITH. Myra!

SIMON. Myra Arundel. I've asked her down.

JUDITH. You've—what!

SIMON. I've asked Myra down for the week-end—she's awfully
amusing.

SOREL. Well, all I can say is, it's beastly of you. You might
have warned me. What on earth will Richard say?

SIMON. Something exquisitely non-committal, I expect.

JUDITH. This is too much! Do you mean to tell me, Simon—

SIMON (*going to Judith; firmly*) Yes, Mother, I do. I've asked
Myra down and I have a perfect right to. You've always brought
us up to be free about things.

JUDITH. Myra Arundel is straining freedom to its *utmost* limits.

SIMON. Don't you like her?

JUDITH. No, dear, I detest her. She's far too old for you, and
she goes about using Sex as a sort of shrimping-net.

SIMON. Really, Mother——!

JUDITH. It's no use being cross. You know perfectly well I dis-
like her, and that's why you never told me she was coming until
too late to stop her. It's intolerable of you.

SOREL (*grandly*) Whether she's here or not is a matter of extreme indifference to *me*, but I'm afraid Richard won't like her very much.

SIMON. You're afraid he'll like her *too* much!

SOREL. That was an offensive remark, Simon, and rather silly.

JUDITH (*plaintively*) Why on earth don't you fall in love with nice young girls, instead of self-conscious vampires?

SIMON. She's not a vampire, and I never said I was in love with her.

SOREL. He's crazy about her. She butters him up and admires his sketches.

SIMON (*leaning across Judith and shouting at Sorel*) What about you picking up old gentlemen at dances?

SOREL (*furiously, shouting back at him*) He's *not* old!

JUDITH (*stretching her arms up and parting them;* SIMON *goes* C) You've both upset me thoroughly. I wanted a nice restful weekend, with moments of Sandy's ingenuous affection to warm the cockles of my heart when I felt in the mood, and now the house is going to be full of discord—not enough food, everyone fighting for the bath—perfect agony! I wish I were dead!

SIMON. You needn't worry about Myra and me. We shall keep out of everyone's way.

SOREL. I shall take Richard on the river all day tomorrow.

JUDITH. In what?

SOREL. The punt.

JUDITH. I absolutely forbid you to go near the punt.

SIMON. It's sure to rain, anyhow.

JUDITH. What your father will say I tremble to think. He needs complete quiet to finish off "The Sinful Woman".

SOREL. I see no reason for there to be any noise, unless Sandy What's-his-name is given to shouting.

JUDITH. If you're rude to Sandy I shall be extremely angry.

(SIMON *and* SOREL *bend over* JUDITH *and all talk loudly at once*)

SOREL SIMON JUDITH } (*together*)	{ Now, look here, Mother—— Why you should expect—— He's coming all the way down specially to be nice to me——

(DAVID *enters down the stairs. He looks slightly irritable*)

DAVID (*coming down to* C) Why are you all making such a noise?

(SIMON *crosses to the piano and picks up a book*)

JUDITH. I think I'm going mad!

DAVID. Why hasn't Clara brought me my tea?

JUDITH. I don't know.

DAVID. Where is Clara?

JUDITH. Do stop firing questions at me, David.

DAVID. Why are you all so irritable? What's happened?

(CLARA *enters from below the stairs, with a tray of tea for one, and thrusts it into* DAVID'S *hands*)

CLARA. Here's your tea. I'm sorry I'm late with it. Amy forgot to put the kettle on—she's got terrible toothache.

DAVID. Poor girl! Give her some oil of cloves.

SOREL. If anyone else mentions oil of cloves, I shall do something desperate! (*She rises and moves a step up* L)

DAVID. It's wonderful stuff. Where's Zoe?

SIMON. She was in the garden this morning.

DAVID. I suppose no-one thought of giving her any lunch?

CLARA. I put it down by the kitchen table as usual, but she never came in for it.

SOREL. She's probably mousing.

DAVID. She isn't old enough yet. She might have fallen into the river, for all you care. I think it's a shame!

CLARA. Don't you worry your head—Zoe won't come to any harm; she's too wily.

(CLARA *exits through the door below the stairs*)

DAVID. I don't want to be disturbed. (*He takes his tray and goes upstairs; then he turns*) Listen, Simon. There's a perfectly sweet flapper coming down by the four-thirty. Will you go and meet her and be nice to her? She's an abject fool, but a useful type, and I want to study her a little in domestic surroundings. She can sleep in the Japanese room.

(DAVID *goes off, leaving behind him a deathly silence.* SOREL *drops into the chair down* L)

JUDITH (*after a pause*) I should like someone to play something very beautiful to me on the piano.

SIMON (*stamps up to the french window* C) Damn everything! Damn! Damn! Damn!

SOREL. Swearing doesn't help.

SIMON. It helps me a lot.

SOREL. What does Father mean by going on like that?

JUDITH. In view of the imminent reception, you'd better go and shave, Simon.

(SIMON *comes down and leans on the piano*)

SOREL (*rising and bursting into tears of rage*) It's perfectly beastly! Whenever I make any sort of plan about anything, it's always done in by someone. I wish I were earning my own living somewhere—a free agent—able to do whatever I liked without being cluttered up and frustrated by the family——

JUDITH (*picturesquely*) It grieves me to hear you say that, Sorel.

SOREL. Don't be infuriating, Mother!

JUDITH (*sadly*) A change has come over my children of late. I have tried to shut my eyes to it, but in vain. At my time of life one must face bitter facts!

SIMON. This is going to be the blackest Saturday-till-Monday we've ever spent!

JUDITH (*tenderly*) Sorel, you mustn't cry.

SOREL. Don't sympathize with me; it's only temper.

JUDITH (*pulling her down on to the sofa beside her*) Put your head on my shoulder, dear.

SIMON (*bitterly*) Your head, like the golden fleece . . .

SOREL (*tearfully*) Richard'll have to have "Little Hell" and that horrible flapper the Japanese room.

JUDITH. Over my dead body!

SIMON (*coming over to Judith*) Mother, what are we to do?

JUDITH (*pulling him down on his knees and placing his head on her right shoulder, and Sorel's head on her left, making a charming little motherly picture*) We must all be very, very kind to everyone!

SIMON. Now then, Mother, none of that!

JUDITH (*aggrieved*) I don't know what you mean, Simon.

SIMON. You were being beautiful and sad.

JUDITH. But I am beautiful and sad.

SIMON. You're not particularly beautiful, darling, and you never were.

JUDITH. Never mind; I made thousands think I was.

SIMON. And as for being sad——

JUDITH (*pushing Simon on the floor*) Now, Simon, I will not be dictated to like this! If I say I'm sad, I *am* sad. You don't understand, because you're precocious and tiresome. . . . There comes a time in all women's lives——

SOREL (*rising and standing at the L corner of the sofa*) Oh dear! (*With a pained expression*)

JUDITH. What did you say, Sorel?

SOREL. I said, "Oh dear!"

JUDITH. Well, please don't say it again, because it annoys me.

SOREL (*smiling*) You're such a lovely hypocrite!

JUDITH (*casting up her eyes*) I don't know what I've done to be cursed with such ungrateful children! It's very cruel at my time of life——

SIMON. There you go again!

JUDITH (*after a pause; inconsequently*) You're getting far too tall, Sorel.

SOREL. Sorry, Mother!

JUDITH. Give me another of those disgusting cigarettes——

(SIMON *rises and goes to the piano—quickly takes a cigarette*)

I don't know where they came from. (*She rises and goes* C)

SIMON (*moving* C *and giving Judith a cigarette*) Here! (*He lights it for her*)

JUDITH. I'm going to forget entirely about all these dreadful people arriving. My mind henceforward shall be a blank on the subject.

SOREL. It's all very fine, Mother, but——

JUDITH. I made a great decision this morning.

SIMON. What kind of decision?

JUDITH. It's a secret.

SOREL. Aren't you going to tell us?

JUDITH. Of course. I meant it was a secret from your father.

SIMON. What is it?

(JUDITH *goes up* C *and looks off* L *to make sure no-one is listening, then returns to* C)

JUDITH. I'm going back to the stage.

SIMON. I knew it! (*He drops on to the form below the piano*)

JUDITH. I'm stagnating here. I won't stagnate as long as there's breath in my body.

SOREL. Do you think it's wise? You retired so very finally last year. What excuse will you give for returning so soon?

JUDITH. My public, dear—letters from my public!

SIMON. Have you had any?

JUDITH. One or two. That's what decided me, really—I ought to have had hundreds.

SOREL (*kneeling on the* R *corner of the sofa*) We'll write some lovely ones, and you can publish them in the papers.

JUDITH. Of course.

SOREL. You will be dignified about it all, won't you, darling?

JUDITH. I'm much more dignified on the stage than in the country—it's my *milieu*. I've tried terribly hard to be "landed gentry", but without any real success. (*She moves up* C *with outstretched arms*) I long for excitement and glamour. (*She comes down to the* R *corner of the sofa*) Think of the thrill of a first night; all those ardent playgoers willing one to succeed; the critics all leaning forward with glowing faces, receptive and exultant—emitting queer little inarticulate noises as some witty line tickles their fancy. The satisfied grunt of the *Daily Mail*, the abandoned gurgle of the *Sunday Times*, and the shrill, enthusiastic scream of the *Daily Express*! I can distinguish them all——

SIMON. Have you got a play?

JUDITH. I think I shall revive *Love's Whirlwind*.

SOREL (*collapsing on to the sofa*) Oh, Mother! (*She gurgles with laughter*)

SIMON (*weakly*) Father will be furious.

JUDITH. I can't help that.

SOREL. It's such a fearful play.

JUDITH. It's a marvellous part.

(SOREL *opens her mouth to speak*)

You mustn't say too much against it, Sorel. I'm willing to laugh at it a little myself, but, after all, it *was* one of my greatest successes.

SIMON. Oh, it's appalling—but I love it. It makes me laugh.

JUDITH. The public love it too, and it doesn't make them laugh —much. (*She moves to* C *and very dramatically recites*) "You are a fool, a blind pitiable fool. You think because you have bought my body that you have bought my soul!" (*Turning to Simon*) You must say that's dramatic—"I've dreamed of love like this, but I never realized, I never knew how beautiful it could be in reality!" (*She wipes away imaginary tears*) That line always brought a tear to my eye.

SIMON. The second act *is* the best, there's no doubt about that.

JUDITH (*turning to Sorel*) From the moment Victor comes in it's strong—tremendously strong . . . Be Victor a minute, Sorel——

SOREL (*rising*) Do you mean when he comes in at the end of the act?

JUDITH. Yes. You know—"Is this a game?"

SOREL (*going to Judith and speaking in a very dramatic voice*) "Is this a game?"

JUDITH (*with spirit*) "Yes—and a game that must be played to the finish."

SIMON (*rising and moving to Judith, and speaking in a deep dramatic voice*) "Zara, what does this mean?"

JUDITH. "So many illusions shattered—so many dreams trodden in the dust!"

SOREL (*running behind Judith and in front of Simon to down* R) I'm George now—"I don't understand! You and Victor—my God!" (*She strikes a dramatic pose*)

JUDITH (*moving a little to* L; *listening*) "Sssh! Isn't that little Pam crying?"

SIMON (*savagely*) "She'll cry more, poor mite, when she realizes her mother is a——"

(*The front-door bell rings*)

JUDITH. Damn! There's the bell!

SOREL (*rushing to the glass on the piano*) I look hideous!

SIMON (*moving to the* R *side of the piano*) Yes, dear!

(CLARA *enters from the door below the stairs and crosses to the door* R)

JUDITH. Clara—before you open the door—we shall be eight for dinner.

CLARA (*coming to* RC) My God!

SIMON. And for breakfast, lunch, tea, and dinner tomorrow.

JUDITH (*vaguely*) Will you get various rooms ready?

CLARA. I shall have to—they can't sleep in the passage!

SOREL. Now we've upset Clara!

JUDITH. It can't be helped—nothing can be helped. It's Fate
—everything that happens is Fate. That's always a great comfort
to me.

CLARA. More like arrant selfishness!

JUDITH. You mustn't be pert, Clara.

CLARA. Pert I may be, but I 'ave got some thought for others.
Eight for dinner—Amy going home early! It's nothing more nor
less than an imposition!

   (*The bell rings again*)

SIMON. Hadn't you better let them all in?

   (CLARA *goes to the front door and admits* SANDY TYRELL, *who is a
fresh-looking young man; he has an unspoilt, youthful sense of honour
and rather big hands, owing to a misplaced enthusiasm for amateur
boxing.* CLARA *goes out, through the door below the stairs*)

SANDY (*crossing to Judith and shaking hands*) I say, it's perfectly
ripping of you to let me come down.

JUDITH. Are you alone?

SANDY (*surprised*) Yes.

JUDITH. I mean, didn't you meet anyone at the station?

SANDY. I motored down; my car's outside. Would you like me
to meet anybody?

JUDITH. Oh, no, I must introduce you. This is my daughter
Sorel, and my son Simon.

SANDY (*moving to* SOREL *and offering his hand, which she ignores*)
How do you do?

SOREL (*coldly*) I'm extremely well, thank you, and I hope you
are.

   (SOREL *brushes past him and exits upstairs*)

SIMON. So do I.

   (SIMON *brushes past him and exits up the stairs.* SANDY *looks
shattered*)

JUDITH (*crossing in front of Sandy and glaring after Simon and Sorel*)
You must forgive me for having rather peculiar children. Have
you got a bag or anything?

SANDY. Yes; it's in the car.

JUDITH. We'd better leave it there for the moment, as Clara
has to get the tea. We'll find you a room afterwards.

SANDY. I've been looking forward to this most awfully.

JUDITH. It is nice, isn't it? (*She moves to the window*) You can see
as far as Marlow on a clear day, so they tell me.

SANDY (*going up to her*) I meant I've been looking forward to
seeing you.

JUDITH. How perfectly sweet of you! (*She crosses to the sofa and
sits* L *on the corner*) Would you like a drink?

SANDY. No, thanks. I'm in training.

JUDITH (*motioning him to sit beside her*) How lovely! What for?

SANDY. I'm boxing again in a couple of weeks.

JUDITH. I must come to your first night.

SANDY (*sitting on the sofa*) You look simply splendid.

JUDITH. I'm so glad. You know, you mustn't mind if Simon and Sorel insult you a little—they've been very bad-tempered lately.

SANDY. It's awfully funny you having a grown-up son and daughter at all. I can hardly believe it.

JUDITH (*quickly*) I was married very young.

SANDY. I don't wonder. You know, it's frightfully queer the way I've been planning to know you for ages, and I never did until last week.

JUDITH. I liked you from the first, really, because you're such a nice shape.

SANDY (*slightly embarrassed*) Oh, I see. . . .

JUDITH. Small hips and lovely broad shoulders—I wish Simon had smaller hips. (*After a slight pause*) Do you think you could teach him to box?

SANDY. Rather—if he likes!

JUDITH. That's just the trouble—I'm afraid he won't like. He's so dreadfully un—that sort of thing. You must use your influence subtly. I'm sure David would be pleased.

SANDY. Who's David?

JUDITH. My husband.

SANDY (*surprised*) Oh!

JUDITH. Why do you say "Oh" like that? Didn't you know I had a husband?

SANDY. I thought he was dead.

JUDITH. No, he's not dead; he's upstairs. (*She points to the stairs*)

SANDY. You're quite different from what you were the other day.

JUDITH. It's this garden hat. I'll take it off. (*She does so and puts it on the table behind the sofa*) There! I've been pruning the calceolarias.

SANDY (*puzzled*) Oh?——

JUDITH. I love my garden, you know—it's so peaceful and quaint. I spend long days dreaming away in it—you know how one dreams.

SANDY. Oh, yes.

JUDITH (*warming up*) I always longed to leave the brittle glamour of cities and theatres and find rest in some old-world nook. That's why we came to Cookham.

SANDY. Awfully nice place, Cookham.

JUDITH (*after a slight pause*) Have you ever seen me on the stage?

SANDY. Rather!

JUDITH. Oh, what in?

SANDY. That thing when you pretended to cheat at cards to save your husband's good name.

JUDITH. Oh, *The Bold Deceiver*. That play was never quite right.

SANDY. You were absolutely wonderful. That was when I first fell in love with you.

JUDITH (*delighted*) Was it, really?

SANDY. Yes; you were so frightfully pathetic and brave.

JUDITH (*basking*) Was I?

SANDY. Rather!

(*There is a pause*)

JUDITH. Well, go on. . . .

SANDY (*flustered*) I feel such a fool, telling you what I think, as though it mattered.

JUDITH. Of course it matters—to me, anyhow.

SANDY. Does it—honestly?

JUDITH. Certainly.

SANDY. It seems too good to be true—sitting here and talking as though we were old friends.

JUDITH. We *are* old friends—we probably met in another life. Reincarnation, you know—fascinating!

SANDY. You do say ripping things.

JUDITH. Do I? Give me a cigarette.

(SANDY *takes a cigarette from the box on the table and gives it to her*)

And let's put our feet up. (*She puts her feet up behind Sandy, and he lights her cigarette*)

SANDY. All right.

(*They settle themselves comfortably at opposite ends of the sofa, smoking*)

JUDITH. Can you punt?

SANDY. Yes—a bit.

JUDITH. You must teach Simon—he always gets the pole stuck.

SANDY. I'd rather teach you.

JUDITH. You're so gallant and chivalrous—much more like an American than an Englishman.

SANDY. I should like to go on saying nice things to you for ever.

JUDITH (*giving him her hand*) Sandy!

(*There comes a loud ring at the bell*)

There now! (*She takes her feet off the sofa*)

SANDY. Is anyone else coming to stay?

JUDITH. Anyone else! You don't know—you just don't know.

(CLARA *enters and crosses over to the door* R, *opens it and lets it fall back in* MYRA's *face, then exits* L)

SANDY. You said it would be quite quiet, with nobody at all.

JUDITH. I was wrong. It's going to be very noisy, with herds of angry people stamping about. Give me my hat.

(SANDY *gives her her hat, which she puts on.*
    MYRA *pushes open the door, puts her suitcase and tennis racket just outside door, and enters, coming to* C *and holding out her hand to Judith.* SANDY *rises*)

MYRA (*advancing*) Judith—my dear—this is divine!

JUDITH (*rising and meeting Myra* C; *emptily*) Too, too lovely! Where are the others?

MYRA. What others?

JUDITH. Did you come by the four-thirty?

MYRA. Yes.

JUDITH. Didn't you see anyone at the station?

MYRA. Yes, several people, but I didn't know they were coming here.

JUDITH. Well, they are.

MYRA. Sorel said it was going to be just ourselves this week-end.

JUDITH (*sharply*) Sorel?

MYRA. Yes—didn't she tell you she'd asked me? Weren't you expecting me?

JUDITH. Simon muttered something about your coming, but Sorel didn't mention it. (*She looks at Myra and gives a chuckle*) Wasn't that odd of her? (*She crosses to the piano*)

MYRA. You're a divinely mad family! (*To Sandy*) How do you do? It's useless to wait for introductions, with the Blisses. My name's Myra Arundel.

JUDITH (*airily*) Sandy Tyrell, Myra Arundel; Myra Arundel, Sandy Tyrell. There!

MYRA. Is that your car outside?

SANDY. Yes.

MYRA (*moving to Judith again*) Well, Judith, I *do* think you might have told me someone was motoring down. A nice car would have been so much more comfortable than that beastly train.

JUDITH. I never knew you were coming until a little while ago.

MYRA. It's heavenly here—after London! The heat was terrible when I left. You look awfully well, Judith. Rusticating obviously agrees with you.

JUDITH. I'm glad you think so. Personally, I feel that a nervous breakdown is imminent.

MYRA. My dear, how ghastly! What's the matter?

JUDITH. Nothing's the matter yet, Myra, but I have presentiments. (*She crosses in front of Myra and takes Sandy's hand. She begins to go upstairs, followed by* SANDY. *Then she turns*) Come upstairs, Sandy, and I'll show you your room. I'll send Simon down to you. He's shaving, I think, but you won't mind that, will you?

(JUDITH *goes off with* SANDY. MYRA *makes a slight grimace after her, then she helps herself to a cigarette and wanders to the piano.* SIMON *comes downstairs very fast, putting on his coat. He has apparently finished his toilet*)

SIMON (*running over to Myra*) Myra, this is marvellous! (*He tries to kiss her*)
MYRA (*pushing him away*) No, Simon, dear; it's too hot.
SIMON. You look beautifully cool.
MYRA. I'm more than cool, really, but it's not climatic coolness. I've been mentally chilled to the marrow by Judith's attitude.
SIMON. Why, what did she say?
MYRA. Nothing very much. She was bouncing about on the sofa with a hearty young thing in flannels, and seemed to resent my appearance rather.
SIMON. You mustn't take any notice of Mother.
MYRA. I'll try not to, but it's difficult.
SIMON. She adores you, really.
MYRA. I'm sure she does.
SIMON. She's annoyed today because Father and Sorel have been asking people down without telling her.
MYRA. Poor dear! I quite see why.
SIMON. You look enchanting!
MYRA. Thank you, Simon.
SIMON. Are you pleased to see me?
MYRA. Of course. That's why I came.
SIMON (*shouting*) Darling!
MYRA. Ssh! Don't shout.
SIMON (*moving away to* C) I feel most colossally temperamental —I should like to kiss you and kiss you and kiss you and break everything in the house and then jump into the river.
MYRA. Dear Simon!
SIMON (*taking her hand and studying her*) You're everything I want you to be—absolutely everything! Marvellous clothes, marvellous looks, marvellous brain—oh, God, it's terrible! (*He drops her hand and moves* L)
MYRA. I dined with Charlie Templeton last night.
SIMON. Well, you're a devil! You only did it to annoy me. He's far too plump, and he can't do anything but dither about the Embassy in badly-cut trousers. You loathe him really; you know you do—you're too intelligent not to. You couldn't like him and me at the same time—it's impossible!
MYRA. Don't be so conceited.
SIMON (*running to her and clasping her in his arms*) Darling—I adore you!
MYRA. That's right.
SIMON (*releasing her*) But you're callous—that's what it is, callous! You don't care a damn. You don't love me a bit, do you?

MYRA. Love's a very big word, Simon.

SIMON. It isn't—it's tiny. What are we to do?

MYRA. What do you mean?

SIMON. We can't go on like this.

MYRA. I'm not going on like anything. (*She crosses over and sits in the chair down* L)

SIMON. Yes, you are; you're going on like Medusa, and there are awful snakes popping their heads out at me from under your hat—I shall be turned to stone in a minute, and then you'll be sorry.

MYRA (*laughing*) You're very sweet, and I'm *very* fond of you.

SIMON (*crossing over to her and taking her hand*) Tell me what you've been doing—everything.

MYRA. Nothing.

SIMON. What did you do after you'd dined with Charlie Templeton?

MYRA. Supped with Charlie Templeton.

SIMON. Well! (*He throws her hand down and goes to the* R *corner of the sofa and sits on the arm*) I don't mind a bit. I hope you ate a lot and enjoyed yourself—there!

MYRA. Generous boy! Come and kiss me.

SIMON. You're only playing up to me now; you don't really want to a bit.

MYRA. I'm aching for it.

SIMON (*running to her and kissing her violently*) I love you!

MYRA. This week-end's going to be strenuous.

SIMON (*moving away to* C) Hell upon earth—fifteen million people in the house. We'll get up at seven and rush away down the river.

MYRA. No, we won't.

SIMON. Well, don't let either of us agree to anything we say— we'll both be difficult. (*He flings himself on the sofa with his feet up on the* L *end*) I love being difficult.

MYRA. You certainly do.

SIMON. But I'm in the most lovely mood now. Just seeing you makes me feel grand——

MYRA. Is your father here?

SIMON. Yes; he's working on a new novel.

MYRA. He writes brilliantly.

SIMON. Doesn't he? He drinks too much tea, though.

MYRA. It can't do him much harm, surely?

SIMON. It tans the stomach.

MYRA. Who is Sandy Tyrell?

SIMON. Never heard of him.

MYRA. He's here, with Judith.

SIMON. Oh, *that* poor thing with hot hands! We'll ignore him.

MYRA. I thought he looked rather nice.

SIMON. You must be mad! He looked disgusting.

MYRA (*laughing*) Idiot!

SIMON. Smooth my hair with your soft white hands.

MYRA (*rising and going to the* R *end of the sofa; ruffling it*) It's got glue on it.

SIMON (*catching her hand and kissing it*) You smell heavenly! What is it?

MYRA. Borgia of Rosine.

SIMON. How appropriate! (*He tries to pull her down and kiss her*)

MYRA (*breaking away*) You're too demonstrative today, Simon.

(*The front-door bell rings*)

SIMON. Damn, damn! It's those drearies. (*He takes his feet off the sofa*)

(CLARA *enters, crosses to the door* R, *opens it and lets it fall back in Richard's face, and starts to return to the door* L, *but stops as he speaks.* RICHARD GREATHAM *and* JACKIE CORYTON *come in. There is, by this time, a good deal of luggage on the step.* RICHARD *is iron-grey and tall;* JACKIE *is small and shingled, with an ingenuous manner which will lose its charm as she grows older*)

RICHARD. Is this Mrs Bliss's house?

CLARA (*off-hand*) Oh, yes, this is it.

RICHARD. Is Miss Sorel Bliss in?

CLARA. I expect so. I'll see if I can find her.

(CLARA *goes upstairs.* RICHARD *closes the door.* JACKIE *goes down* R)

SIMON (*rising and crossing to Richard, carelessly shaking hands, then turning back to Myra, ignoring Richard*) Hallo! Did you have a nice journey?

RICHARD. Yes, thank you, very nice. I met Miss Coryton at the station. We introduced ourselves while we were waiting for the only taxi to come back.

MYRA (*taking a step down* LC) Oh, *I* took the only taxi. How maddening of me!

RICHARD (*crossing to her and shaking hands*) Mrs Arundel! How do you do? I never recognized you.

(SIMON *goes behind Richard to* RC *and stares at Jackie rudely*)

JACKIE. I did.

MYRA. Why? Have we met anywhere?

JACKIE. No; I mean I recognized you as the one who took the taxi.

RICHARD (*to Simon*) You are Sorel's brother?

SIMON. Yes; she'll be down in a minute. Come out into the garden, Myra——

MYRA. But, Simon, we can't . . .

SIMON (*reaching across Richard, grabbing Myra's hand and dragging her off through the window*) Yes, we can. I shall go mad if I stay in the house a moment longer. (*Over his shoulder to Richard and Jackie*) Tea will be here soon.

(SIMON *and* MYRA *go off into the garden* R. *There is a slight pause*)

JACKIE. Well!

RICHARD. A strange young man! (*He moves up to the window, looking after them*)

JACKIE. Very rude, *I* think.

RICHARD (*turning back into the room*) Have you ever met him before?

JACKIE. No; I don't know any of them except Mr Bliss--he's a wonderful person.

RICHARD (*putting his coat and hat on the chair up* LC) I wonder if he knows you're here.

JACKIE. Perhaps that funny woman who opened the door will tell him.

RICHARD. Yes, allow me. (*He takes Jackie's coat and puts it on the chair with his*) It was fortunate that we met at the station.

JACKIE. I'm frightfully glad. I should have been terrified arriving all by myself.

RICHARD (*looking out of the window again; after a slight pause*) I do hope the weather will keep good over Sunday—the country round here is delightful.

JACKIE. Yes.

(*Another pause*)

RICHARD. There's nowhere like England in the spring and summer.

JACKIE. No, there isn't, is there?

(*Another pause*)

RICHARD. There's a sort of *quality* you find in no other countries.

(*There is another pause, in which* JACKIE *moves over to the sofa and sits*)

JACKIE. Have you travelled a lot?

RICHARD (*modestly*) A good deal.

JACKIE. How lovely!

(RICHARD *comes down and sits on the form below the piano. There is a pause*)

RICHARD. Spain is very beautiful.

JACKIE. Yes, I've always heard Spain was awfully nice.

(*Pause*)

RICHARD. Except for the bull-fights. No-one who ever really loved horses could enjoy a bull-fight.

JACKIE. Nor anyone who loved bulls either.
RICHARD. Exactly.

(*Pause*)

JACKIE. Italy's awfully nice, isn't it?
RICHARD. Oh, yes, charming.
JACKIE. I've always wanted to go to Italy.

(*Pause*)

RICHARD. Rome is a beautiful city.
JACKIE. Yes, I've always heard Rome was lovely.
RICHARD. And Naples and Capri—Capri's enchanting.
JACKIE. It must be.

(*Pause*)

RICHARD. Have you ever been abroad at all?
JACKIE. Oh, yes; I went to Dieppe once—we had a house there
for the summer.
RICHARD (*kindly*) Dear little place, Dieppe.
JACKIE. Yes, it was lovely.

(JUDITH *comes downstairs, followed by* SANDY, *with his arms full of
cushions. She sits down on the form and puts on her goloshes beside*
RICHARD, *who rises. She then exits into the garden without looking at
Richard or Jackie.* SANDY *picks up the cushions and her gloves from
the table and goes out after her*)

JACKIE. Well!

(*Pause.* RICHARD *sits again*)

RICHARD. *Russia* used to be a wonderful country before the
war.
JACKIE. It must have been . . . Was that her?
RICHARD. Who?
JACKIE. Judith Bliss.
RICHARD. Yes, I expect it was.
JACKIE (*nearly crying*) I wish I'd never come.
RICHARD. You mustn't worry. They're a very Bohemian
family, I believe.
JACKIE. I wonder if Mr Bliss knows I'm here.
RICHARD. I wonder.
JACKIE. Couldn't we ring a bell, or anything?
RICHARD. Yes, perhaps we'd better. (*He rises and crosses to the
door down* L. *He finds the bell and presses it*)
JACKIE. I don't suppose it rings.
RICHARD (*coming to the* L *corner of the sofa*) You mustn't be
depressed.
JACKIE. I feel horrid.

RICHARD. It's always a little embarrassing coming to a strange house for the first time. You'll like Sorel—she's charming.

JACKIE (*desperately*) I wonder where she is.

RICHARD (*consolingly*) I expect tea will be here soon.

JACKIE. Do you think they *have* tea?

RICHARD (*alarmed*) Oh, yes—they must.

JACKIE. Oh, well, we'd better go on waiting, then.

RICHARD (*taking his cigarette-case out of his pocket*) Do you mind if I smoke?

JACKIE. Not a bit.

RICHARD. Will you?

JACKIE. No, thank you.

RICHARD (*sitting down on the L end of the sofa*) I got this case in Japan. It's pretty, isn't it?

JACKIE (*taking the case, turning it over and handing it back*) Awfully pretty.

(*They lapse into hopeless silence.* SOREL *enters downstairs, and comes to* LC)

SOREL. Oh, Richard, I'm dreadfully sorry! I didn't know you were here.

(*They shake hands*)

RICHARD. We've been here a good while.

SOREL. How awful! Please forgive me. I was upstairs.

(JACKIE *bobs up under their hands and stands in front of Richard*)

RICHARD. This is Miss Coryton.

SOREL. Oh!

JACKIE. How do you do?

SOREL. Have you come to see Father?

(RICHARD *lights his cigarette*)

JACKIE. Yes.

SOREL. He's in his study. (*She moves away to* C) You'd better go up.

JACKIE (*looking hopelessly at Richard, then going to Sorel and clutching her arm*) I don't know the way.

SOREL (*irritably*) Oh, well—I'll take you. Come on! Wait a minute, Richard. (*She takes Jackie to the bottom of the stairs*) It's along that passage and the third door on the right.

JACKIE. Oh, thank you. (*She goes upstairs despondently*)

SOREL (*coming down again; to Richard*) The poor girl looks half-witted.

RICHARD. She's shy, I think.

SOREL. I hope Father will find her a comfort. (*She sits on the* R *end of the sofa*)

RICHARD. Tell me one thing, Sorel, did your father and mother know I was coming? (*He sits beside her*)

SOREL. Oh, yes; they were awfully pleased.

RICHARD. A rather nice-looking woman came down, in a big hat, and went into the garden with a young man, without saying a word.

SOREL. That was Mother, I expect. We're an independent family—we entertain our friends sort of separately.

RICHARD. Oh, I see.

(*There is a slight pause*)

SOREL. It was sweet of you to come.

RICHARD. I wanted to come—I've thought about you a lot.

SOREL. Have you really? That's thrilling!

RICHARD. I mean it. You're so alive and vital and different from other people.

SOREL. I'm so frightened that you'll be bored here.

RICHARD. Bored! Why should I be?

SOREL. Oh, I don't know. But you won't be, will you?—or if you are, tell me at once, and we'll do something quite different.

RICHARD. You're rather a dear, you know.

SOREL. I'm not. (*She rises and goes* c) I'm devastating, entirely lacking in restraint. So's Simon. It's Father and Mother's fault, really; you see, they're so vague—they've spent their lives culti- vating their Arts and not devoting any time to ordinary conven- tions and manners and things. I'm the only one who sees that, so I'm trying to be better. I'd love to be beautifully poised and carry off difficult situations with a lift of the eyebrows——

RICHARD. I'm sure you could carry off anything.

SOREL (*moving to the* R *corner of the sofa*) There you are, you see, saying the right thing! You *always* say the right thing, and no-one knows a bit what you're really thinking. That's what I adore.

RICHARD. I'm afraid to say anything now, in case you think I'm only being correct.

SOREL. But you are correct. I wish you'd teach Simon to be correct too. (*She sits beside Richard again*)

RICHARD. It would be uphill work, I'm afraid.

SOREL. Why, don't you like him?

RICHARD. I've only met him for a moment.

(*There is an uncomfortable pause*)

SOREL. Would you like to see the garden?

RICHARD (*he half rises*) Very much indeed.

SOREL. No, as a matter of fact——

(RICHARD *sits again*)

we'd better wait until after tea.

(*There is another pause*)

Shall I sing you something?

RICHARD. Please—I should love it.

(*They both rise.* SOREL *goes reluctantly to the piano*)

SOREL (*coming slowly to the sofa*) I don't want to really a bit—only I'm trying to entertain you. It's as easy as pie to talk in someone else's house, like at the dance the other night, but here on my own *ground* I'm finding it difficult.

RICHARD (*puzzled*) I'm sorry.

SOREL. Oh, it isn't your fault; honestly, it isn't—you're awfully kind and responsive. (*She sits on the sofa*) What shall we do?

RICHARD. I'm quite happy talking (*he sits beside her*) to you.

(*Pause*)

SOREL. Can you play Mah Jong?

RICHARD. No, I'm afraid I can't.

SOREL. I'm *so* glad—I *do* hate it so.

(CLARA *enters, with a small stool for tea, and places it with a bang at Richard's feet*)

Here's tea!

CLARA. Where's your mother, dear?

SOREL. Out in the garden, I think.

CLARA. It's starting to rain.

(*She goes out* L *and fetches a tea-tray loaded with tea-things, which she puts on the stool*)

SOREL. Oh, everyone will come dashing in, then. How awful!

RICHARD (*rising and goes* C) Won't the luggage get rather wet out there?

SOREL. What luggage?

CLARA. I'll bring it in when I've made the tea.

RICHARD (*going out* R *and returning with two suitcases, which he places down* RC) Oh, don't trouble; I'll do it now.

SOREL. We ought to have got William up from the village.

CLARA. It's Saturday.

SOREL. I know it is.

CLARA. He's playing cricket.

(SOREL *rushes to help Richard*)

SOREL. Do sit down and smoke. I can easily manage it.

RICHARD. Certainly not.

SOREL (*going out*) How typical of Myra to have so many bags . . . Ooh! (*She staggers with a suitcase*)

(RICHARD *goes to her assistance, and they both drop it*)

There now—we've probably broken something!

RICHARD. Well, it's not my bag, so it doesn't matter.

(RICHARD *goes out to get the last case while* SOREL *holds the door open*)

RICHARD. This is the last one . . . (*He brings in a dressing-case, and wipes his hand on his handkerchief*)

SOREL. Do you know where to wash if you want to?

RICHARD. No—but I'm all right.

(*They both stand leaning on the piano, talking.*
CLARA *enters with a teapot. She puts it on the stool and exits again.*
SIMON *and* MYRA *come in from the garden.* MYRA *goes to shake hands with Sorel, but* SIMON *pulls her towards the sofa*)

MYRA. Hallo, Sorel! How are you?

SOREL. I'm splendid. Do you know Mr Greatham?

MYRA. Oh, yes; we've met several times.

SIMON. Come and sit down, Myra.

(MYRA, *pulled by* SIMON, *sits on the* L *side of the sofa*, SIMON *on the* R *side.*
DAVID *and* JACKIE *come downstairs*, DAVID *leading her by the elbow like a small child. They come* C)

DAVID. Is tea ready?

SOREL. Yes; just.

DAVID (*leaving* JACKIE RC *and crossing to Simon*) Simon, come and be nice to Miss Coryton.

SIMON. We've met already.

DAVID (*dragging him out of his seat, and sitting there himself*) That's no reason for you not to be nice to her.

MYRA (*firmly*) How do you do?

DAVID. How do you do? Are you staying here?

MYRA. I hope so.

(SIMON *moves round to behind the* L *corner of the sofa and sits on the table*)

DAVID. You must forgive me for being rather frowsy, but I've been working hard.

SOREL. Father, this is Mr Greatham.

(RICHARD *takes a step down* R)

DAVID. How are you? When did you arrive?

RICHARD. This afternoon.

DAVID. Good. Have some tea. (*He begins to pour it out*) Everyone had better put their own sugar and milk in, or we shall get muddled. Where's your Mother, Simon?

SIMON (*moving round and taking a cup of tea and a piece of cake, then returning to his seat*) She was last seen in the punt.

DAVID. How extraordinary! She can't punt.

SOREL. Sandy Tyrell's with her.

DAVID. Oh, well, she'll be all right, then. (*After a slight pause*) Who is he?

SOREL. I don't know.

DAVID. Do sit down, everybody.

(JACKIE *sits on the form below the piano. Enter* JUDITH *and* SANDY *from the garden.* JUDITH *comes to* C *and kicks off goloshes*)

JUDITH. There's going to be a thunderstorm. I felt sick this morning. This is Sandy Tyrell—everybody——

SOREL. Mother, I want you to meet Mr Greatham.

(RICHARD *goes to her and shakes hands, then returns to the piano*)

JUDITH. Oh, yes. You were here before, weren't you?

SOREL. Before *what*, darling?

(SOREL *crosses and gets a cup of tea and returns with it to the settee down* R)

JUDITH. Before I went out in the punt. There was somebody else here, too—a fair girl. (*She sees Jackie*) Oh, there you are! How do you do? Sit down, Sandy, and eat anything you want. Give Sandy some bread-and-butter, Simon. (*She crosses* L *and helps herself to tea, then sits in the chair down* L)

(RICHARD *and* JACKIE *sit on the form below the piano.* SANDY *remains standing* C)

SIMON (*rising, picking up the plate of bread-and-butter, crossing to Sandy and ungraciously thrusting it into his hands, then returning to his seat*) Here you are!

SANDY. Thanks.

(*There is a long pause; then* MYRA *and* RICHARD *speak together*)

| RICHARD | | How far are you from Maidenhead, exactly? |
| MYRA | (*together*) | What a pity it's raining—we might have had some tennis—— |

(*They both stop, to let the other go on. There is another terrible silence*)

| MYRA | | I adore the shape of this hall—it's so—— |
| RICHARD | (*together*) | The train was awfully crowded coming down—— |

They both stop again, and there is another dead silence, during which—

the CURTAIN *slowly falls*

ACT II

SCENE—*The same. It is after dinner on the Saturday evening.*

When the CURTAIN *rises* DAVID *and* MYRA *are seated on the settee down*
R. SANDY *and* JACKIE *are seated on the form below the piano.* SOREL
is standing down C, *with her back to the audience.* SIMON *is seated on*
the R *arm of the sofa.* RICHARD *is seated on the sofa.* JUDITH *is seated*
in the chair down L. *Everyone is talking and arguing. The following*
scene should be played with great speed.

SIMON. Who'll go out?

SOREL. I don't mind.

SIMON. No; you always guess it too quickly.

JACKIE. What do we have to do?

JUDITH. Choose an adverb, and then——

SIMON. Someone goes out, you see, and comes in, and you've
chosen a word among yourselves, and she or he, whoever it is,
asks you some sort of question, and you have to——

SOREL (*moving up to Simon*) Not an ordinary question, Simon;
they have to ask them to do something in the manner of the word,
and then——

SIMON. Then, you see, you act whatever it is——

SOREL. The answer to the question, you see?

RICHARD (*apprehensively*) What sort of thing is one expected
to do?

JUDITH. Quite unusual things, like reciting *If*, or playing the
piano——

RICHARD. I can't play the piano.

SIMON. Never mind; you can fake it, as long as it conveys an
idea of the word.

JACKIE. The word we've all thought of?

SOREL (*impatiently*) Yes, the word we've chosen when whoever
it is is out of the room.

JACKIE. I'm afraid I don't quite understand yet.

SIMON. Never mind; I'll explain. You see, someone goes
out . . .

SOREL. I'll go out the first time, just to show her.

JUDITH. It's quite simple—all you have to do is just act in the
manner of the word.

SOREL. Look here, everybody, I'm going out.

SIMON. All right; go on.

(SOREL *moves to the door down* L *but stops in the doorway as* MYRA
speaks)

MYRA. The History game's awfully good—when two people

go out, and come back as Mary Queen of Scots and Crippen or somebody.

SANDY (*despondently*) I'm no earthly good at this sort of thing.

SOREL. I'll show you, Sandy. You see . . .

JUDITH. There's always "How, When, and Where?" We haven't played that for ages.

SIMON. We will afterwards. We'll do this one first. Go on, Sorel.

SOREL. Don't be too long.

(SOREL *goes out through the door down* L)

SIMON (*rising and facing the company*) Now then.

JUDITH. "Bitterly."

SIMON. No, we did that last week; she'll know.

DAVID. "Intensely."

JUDITH. Too difficult.

RICHARD. There was an amusing game I played once at the Harringtons' house. Everyone was blindfolded except——

SIMON (*going back to the corner of the sofa*) This room's not big enough for that. What about "winsomely"?

JACKIE. I wish I knew what we had to do.

JUDITH. You'll see when we start playing.

MYRA (*rising and crossing to the table behind the sofa, taking a cigarette and lighting it*) *If* we start playing.

SIMON. Mother's brilliant at this. Do you remember when we played it at the Mackenzies'?

JUDITH. Yes, and Blanche was so cross when I kissed Freddie's ear in the manner of the word.

RICHARD. What was the word?

JUDITH. I can't remember.

MYRA (*having lit the cigarette she returns to her seat*) Perhaps it's as well.

DAVID. What about "drearily"?

JUDITH. Not definite enough.

SIMON. "Winsomely" is the best.

JUDITH. She's sure to guess it straight off.

SANDY (*confidentially to Jackie*) These games are much too brainy for me.

DAVID. Young Norman Robertson used to be marvellous—do you remember?

SIMON. Yes, wonderful sense of humour.

MYRA. He's lost it all since his marriage.

JUDITH. I didn't know you knew him.

MYRA. Well, considering he married my cousin——

(*There is a pause*)

RICHARD. We don't seem to be getting on with the game.

JUDITH. We haven't thought of a word yet.

Myra. "Brightly."

Simon. Too obvious.

Myra. Very well—don't snap at me!

Judith. "Saucily." I've got a lovely idea for "saucily."

Myra (*to Simon*) I should think "rudely" would be the easiest.

Simon. Don't be sour, Myra.

Judith. The great thing is to get an obscure word.

Simon. What a pity Irene isn't here—she knows masses of obscure words.

Myra. She's probably picked them up from her obscure friends.

Simon. It's no use being catty about Irene; she's a perfect darling.

Myra. I wasn't being catty at all.

Simon. Yes, you were.

Sorel (*off*) Hurry up!

Judith. Quickly, now! We must think——

Jackie (*rising and coming* c; *helpfully*) "Appendicitis."

Judith (*witheringly*) That's not an adverb.

Simon. You're thinking of Charades.

(Jackie *returns to her seat*)

Sandy. Charades are damned good fun.

Simon. Yes, but we don't happen to be doing them at the moment.

Sandy. Sorry.

Judith. "Saucily."

Simon. No, "winsomely" is better.

Judith. All right. Call her in.

Simon (*calling*) Sorel—come on; we're ready.

Sandy (*hoarsely to Simon*) Which is it—"saucily" or "winsomely"?

Simon (*whispering*) "Winsomely."

(Sorel *enters. She moves to* c)

Sorel (*to Judith*) Go and take a flower out of that vase and give it to Richard.

Judith. Very well.

(Judith *trips lightly over to the vase on the piano, gurgling with coy laughter, selects a flower, then goes over to Richard; pursing her lips into a mock smile, she gives him the flower with a little girlish gasp at her own daring and wags her finger archly at him, and returns to her seat.* Richard *puts the flower on the sofa table and sits again*)

Simon. Marvellous, Mother!

Sorel (*laughing*) Oh, lovely! (*Looking round the company*) Now, Myra, get up and say good-bye to everyone in the manner of the word.

MYRA (*rising and starting with David*) Good-bye. It really has been most delightful——
JUDITH. No, no, no!
MYRA (*moving* C) Why—what do you mean?
JUDITH. You haven't got the right intonation a bit.
SIMON. Oh, Mother darling, do shut up!
MYRA (*acidly*) Remember what an advantage you have over we poor amateurs, Judith, having been a professional for so long. (*She returns to her seat*)
JUDITH. I don't like "so long" very much.
SOREL. Do you think we might go on now?
MYRA. Go to the next one; I'm not going to do any more.
SIMON. Oh, please do. You were simply splendid.
SOREL. It doesn't matter. (*To Richard*) Light a cigarette in the manner of the word.

(RICHARD *rises*)

RICHARD (*taking a cigarette from the box on the sofa table*) I've forgotten what it is.
JUDITH (*grimacing at him violently*) You remember . . .
RICHARD. Oh, yes.

(RICHARD *goes to Sorel* C *and proceeds to light a cigarette with great abandon, winking his eye and chucking Sorel under the chin, then looks round panic-stricken*)

JUDITH. Oh, no, no, no!
MYRA. I can't think *what* that's meant to be.
RICHARD (*offended*) I was doing my best.
JUDITH. It's so *frightfully* easy, and nobody can do it right.
SIMON. I believe you've muddled it up.
RICHARD (*returning to his seat*) You'd better go to the next one.
JUDITH. Which word were you doing? Whisper——
RICHARD (*leaning over to her, whispering*) "Saucily."
JUDITH. I knew it!—he was doing the wrong word. (*She whispers to him*)
RICHARD. Oh, I see. I'm so sorry.
JUDITH. Give him another chance.
SIMON. No, it's Jackie's turn now; it will come round to him again, I'm afraid.
SOREL (*moving to Jackie*) Do a dance in the manner of the word.
JACKIE (*giggling*) I can't.
JUDITH. Nonsense! Of course you can.
JACKIE. I can't—honestly—I
SIMON (*crossing and pulling her to her feet*) Go on; have a shot at it.
JACKIE. No, I'd much rather not. Count me out.
JUDITH. Really, the ridiculous fuss everyone makes——

JACKIE. I'm awfully stupid at anything like this.

SOREL. It's only a game, after all.

DAVID. Come along—try.

JACKIE (*dragging back*) I couldn't—please don't ask me to. I simply couldn't. (*She sits again*)

SIMON. Leave her alone if she doesn't want to.

SOREL (*irritably*) What's the use of playing at all, if people won't do it properly!

JUDITH. It's *so* simple.

SANDY. It's awfully difficult if you haven't done it before.

SIMON. Go on to the next one.

SOREL (*firmly*) Unless everyone's in it we won't play at all.

SIMON. Now, don't lose your temper.

SOREL. Lose my temper! I like that! No-one's given me the slightest indication of what the word is—you all argue and squabble——

DAVID. Talk, talk, talk! Everybody talks too much.

JUDITH. It's so surprising to me when people won't play up. After all——

JACKIE (*with spirit*) It's a hateful game, anyhow, and I don't want to play it again ever.

SOREL. You haven't played it at all yet.

SIMON. Don't be rude, Sorel.

SOREL. Really, Simon, the way you go on is infuriating!

SIMON. It's always the same; whenever Sorel goes out she gets quarrelsome.

SOREL. Quarrelsome!

SIMON (*patting Jackie's hand in a fatherly fashion*) Don't worry, Jackie; you needn't do anything you don't want to.

JUDITH. I think, for the future, we'd better confine our efforts to social conversation and not attempt anything in the least intelligent.

SIMON. How can you be so unkind, Mother!

JUDITH (*sharply*) Don't speak to me like that!

JACKIE (*speaking winsomely*) It's all my fault—I know I'm awfully silly, but it embarrasses me so terribly doing anything in front of people.

SOREL (*with acidity*) I should think the word was "winsomely".

SIMON. You must have been listening outside the door, then.

SOREL. Not at all—Miss Coryton gave it away.

SIMON. Why "Miss Coryton" all of a sudden? You've been calling her Jackie all the evening. You're far too grand, Sorel.

SOREL (*stamping her foot*) And you're absolutely maddening— I'll never play another game with you as long as I live!

SIMON. That won't break my heart.

JUDITH. Stop, stop, stop!

SIMON (*grabbing Jackie's hand and pulling her up to the window*) Come out in the garden. I'm sick of this.

SOREL (*following them up and shouting after them*) Don't let him take you on the river; he isn't very good at it.

SIMON (*over his shoulder*) Ha, ha!—very funny!

(SIMON *drags* JACKIE *off.* SOREL *returns to* C)

JUDITH. Sorel, you're behaving disgracefully.

SOREL. Simon ought to go into the army, or something.

DAVID. You both ought to be in reformatories.

SOREL. This always happens whenever we play a game. We're a beastly family, and I hate us.

JUDITH. Speak for yourself, dear.

SOREL. I can't, without speaking for everyone else too—we're all exactly the same, and I'm ashamed of us.

(SOREL *grasps* SANDY's *hand and drags him off through the door* L)

Come into the library, Sandy.

MYRA (*rising and going to the table behind the sofa*) Charming! It's all perfectly charming!

DAVID (*rising and standing* RC) I think it would be better, Judith, if you exercised a little more influence over the children.

JUDITH. That's right—blame it all on me.

DAVID. After all, dear, you started it, by snapping everybody up.

JUDITH (*rising and crossing to him*) You ought never to have married me, David; it was a great mistake.

DAVID. The atmosphere of this house is becoming more unbearable every day, and all because Simon and Sorel are allowed to do exactly what they like.

JUDITH. You sit upstairs all day, writing your novels.

DAVID. Novels which earn us our daily bread.

JUDITH. "Daily bread"—nonsense! (*She crosses down* R) We've got enough money to keep us in comfort until we die.

DAVID. That will be very soon, if we can't get a little peace. (*To Myra*) Come out into the garden——

(*They both go up to the window*)

JUDITH. I sincerely hope the night air will cool you.

DAVID (*coming down to Judith*) I don't know what's happened to you, lately, Judith.

JUDITH. Nothing's happened to me—nothing ever does. You're far too smug to allow it.

DAVID. Smug! Thank you.

JUDITH. Yes, smug, smug, smug! And pompous!

DAVID. I hope you haven't been drinking, dear?

JUDITH. Drinking! (*She laughs*) Huh! that's very amusing!

DAVID. I think it's rather tragic, at your time of life.

(DAVID *goes out with* MYRA. JUDITH *goes after them as if to speak, changes her mind, and comes down to the* L *corner of the sofa*)

JUDITH. David's been a good husband to me, but he's wearing a bit thin now.

RICHARD (*rising*) Would you like me to go? To leave you alone for a little?

JUDITH. Why? Are you afraid I shall become violent?

RICHARD (*smiling*) No; I merely thought perhaps I was in the way.

JUDITH. I hope you're not embarrassed—I couldn't bear you to be embarrassed.

RICHARD. Not in the least.

JUDITH. Marriage is a hideous affair altogether, don't you think?

RICHARD. I'm really hardly qualified to judge, you see——

JUDITH. Do stop being non-committal, just for once; it's doubly annoying in the face of us all having lost control so lamentably.

RICHARD. I'm sorry.

JUDITH. There's nothing to be sorry for, really, because, after all, it's your particular "thing", isn't it?—observing everything and not giving yourself away an inch.

RICHARD. I suppose it is.

JUDITH. You'll get used to us in time, and then you'll feel cosier. Why don't you sit down? (*She sits on the sofa*)

RICHARD (*sitting beside her*) I'm enjoying myself very much.

JUDITH. It's very sweet of you to say so, but I don't see how you can be.

RICHARD (*laughing suddenly*) But I am!

JUDITH. There now, that was quite a genuine laugh! We're getting on. Are you in love with Sorel?

RICHARD (*surprised and embarrassed*) In love with Sorel?

JUDITH (*repentantly*) Now I've killed it—I've murdered the little tender feeling of comfort that was stealing over you, by sheer tactlessness! Will you teach me to be tactful?

RICHARD. Did you really think I was in love with Sorel?

JUDITH. It's so difficult to tell, isn't it?—I mean, you might not know yourself. She's very attractive.

RICHARD. Yes, she is—very.

JUDITH. Have you heard her sing?

RICHARD. No, not yet.

JUDITH. She sings beautifully. Are you susceptible to music?

RICHARD. I'm afraid I don't know very much about it.

JUDITH. You probably are, then. I'll sing you something.

RICHARD. Please do.

JUDITH (*rising and crossing to the piano; he rises and stands* c) It's awfully sad for a woman of my temperament to have a grown-up daughter, you know. I have to put my pride in my pocket and develop in her all the charming little feminine tricks which will eventually cut me out altogether.

RICHARD. That wouldn't be possible.

JUDITH. I do hope you meant that, because it was a sweet remark. (*She is at the piano, turning over music*)

RICHARD (*crossing to the piano*) Of course I meant it.

JUDITH. Will you lean on the piano in an attentive attitude? It's such a help.

RICHARD (*leaning on the piano*) You're an extraordinary person.

JUDITH (*beginning to play*) In what way extraordinary?

RICHARD. When I first met Sorel, I guessed what you'd be like.

JUDITH. Did you, now? And am I?

RICHARD (*smiling*) Exactly.

JUDITH. Oh, well! . . . (*She plays and sings a little French song*)

(*There is a slight pause when it is finished*)

RICHARD (*with feeling*) Thank you.

JUDITH (*rising from the piano*) It's pretty, isn't it?

RICHARD. Perfectly enchanting.

JUDITH (*crossing to the sofa*) Shall we sit down again? (*She re-seats herself on the sofa*)

RICHARD (*moving over to her*) Won't you sing any more?

JUDITH. No, no more—I want you to talk to me and tell me all about yourself, and the things you've done.

RICHARD (*sitting beside her*) I've done nothing.

JUDITH. What a shame! Why not?

RICHARD. I never realize how *dead* I am until I meet people like you. It's depressing, you know.

JUDITH. What nonsense! You're not a bit dead.

RICHARD. Do you always live here?

JUDITH. I'm going to, from now onwards. I intend to sink into a very beautiful old age. When the children marry, I shall wear a cap.

RICHARD (*smiling*) How absurd!

JUDITH. I don't mean a funny cap.

RICHARD. You're far too full of vitality to sink into anything.

JUDITH. It's entirely spurious vitality. If you troubled to look below the surface, you'd find a very wistful and weary spirit. I've been battling with life for a long time.

RICHARD. Surely such successful battles as yours have been are not wearying?

JUDITH. Yes, they are—frightfully. I've reached an age now when I just want to sit back and let things go on around me— and they do.

RICHARD. I should like to know exactly what you're thinking about—really.

JUDITH. I was thinking of calling you Richard. It's such a nice uncompromising name.

RICHARD. I should be very flattered if you would.

JUDITH. I won't suggest you calling me Judith until you feel really comfortable about me.

RICHARD. But I do—Judith.

JUDITH. I'm awfully glad. Will you give me a cigarette?

RICHARD (*producing his case*) Certainly.

JUDITH (*taking one*) Oh, what a divine case!

RICHARD. It was given to me in Japan three years ago. All those little designs mean things.

JUDITH (*bending over it*) What sort of things?

(RICHARD *lights her cigarette*)

RICHARD. Charms for happiness, luck, and—love.

JUDITH. Which is the charm for love?

RICHARD. That one.

JUDITH. What a dear!

(RICHARD *kisses her gently on the neck*)

(*She sits upright, with a scream*) Richard!

RICHARD (*stammering*) I'm afraid I couldn't help it.

JUDITH (*dramatically*) What are we to do? What are we to do?

RICHARD. I don't know.

JUDITH (*rising, thrusting the case in his hand and crossing to* RC) David must be told—everything!

RICHARD (*alarmed*) Everything?

JUDITH (*enjoying herself*) Yes, yes. There come moments in life when it is necessary to be honest—absolutely honest. I've trained myself always to shun the underhand methods other women so often employ—the truth must be faced fair and square——

RICHARD (*extremely alarmed*) The truth? I don't quite understand. (*He rises*)

JUDITH. Dear Richard, you want to spare me, I know—you're so chivalrous; but it's no use. After all, as I said before, David has been a good husband to me, according to his lights. This may, of course, break him up rather, but it can't be helped. I wonder—oh, I wonder how he'll take it! They say suffering's good for writers, it strengthens their psychology. Oh, my poor, poor David! Never mind. You'd better go out into the garden and wait——

RICHARD (*flustered*) Wait? What for? (*He moves to* C)

JUDITH. For me, Richard, for me. I will come to you later. Wait in the summer-house. I had begun to think that Romance was dead, that I should never know it again. Before, of course, I had my work and my life in the theatre, but now, nothing—nothing! Everything is empty and hollow, like a broken shell. (*She sinks on to the form below the piano, and looks up at Richard with a tragic smile, then looks quickly away*)

RICHARD. Look here, Judith, I apologize for what I did just now. I——

JUDITH (*ignoring all interruption, rising and crossing to* LC) But now you have come, and it's all changed—it's magic! I'm under a spell that I never thought to recapture again. Go along——
(*She pushes him towards the garden*)

Richard (*protesting*) But, Judith——

Judith (*pushing him firmly until he is off*) Don't—don't make it any harder for me. I am quite resolved—and it's the only possible way. Go, go!

(Judith *pushes him into the garden and waves to him bravely with her handkerchief; then she comes back into the room and powders her nose before the glass and pats her hair into place. Then, assuming an expression of restrained tragedy, she opens the library door, screams and recoils genuinely shocked to* c. *After a moment or two,* Sorel *and* Sandy *come out rather sheepishly and stand* lc)

Sorel. Look here, Mother, I——

Judith. Sorel, what am I to say to you?

Sorel. I don't know, Mother.

Judith. Neither do I.

Sandy. It was my fault, Mrs Bliss—Judith——

Judith. What a fool I've been! What a blind fool!

Sorel. Mother, are you *really* upset?

Judith (*with feeling*) I'm stunned!

Sorel. But, darling——

Judith (*gently*) Don't speak for a moment, Sorel; we must all be very quiet, and think——

Sorel. It was nothing, really. For heaven's sake——

Judith. Nothing! I open the library door casually, and what do I see? I ask you, what do I see?

Sandy. I'm most awfully sorry. . . .

Judith. Ssshh! It has gone beyond superficial apologies.

Sorel. Mother, be natural for a moment.

Judith. I don't know what you mean, Sorel. I'm trying to realize a very bitter truth as calmly as I can.

Sorel. There's nothing so very bitter about it.

Judith. My poor child!

Sorel (*suddenly*) Very well, then! I love Sandy, and he loves me!

Judith. That is the only possible excuse for your behaviour.

Sorel. Why shouldn't we love each other if we want to?

Judith. Sandy was in love with me this afternoon.

Sorel. Not real love—you know it wasn't.

Judith (*bitterly*) I know now.

Sandy (*crossing to* l *of Judith*) I say—look here—I'm most awfully sorry.

Judith. There's nothing to be sorry for, really; it's my fault for having been so—so ridiculous.

Sorel. Mother!

Judith (*sadly*) Yes, ridiculous. (*She goes up to the piano*) I'm getting old, old, and the sooner I face it the better. (*She picks up the mirror, looks at herself, and puts it down again quickly*)

SOREL (*hopelessly*) But, darling . . .

JUDITH (*splendidly, going to Sorel*) Youth will be served. You're so pretty, Sorel, far prettier than I ever was—I'm very glad you're pretty.

SANDY (*moving down* R) I feel a fearful cad.

JUDITH. Why should you? You've answered the only call that really counts—the call of Love, and Romance, and Spring. I forgive you, Sandy, completely. There! (*She goes to him and pats his shoulder*)

SOREL. Well, that's all right, then. (*She sits on the sofa*)

JUDITH. I resent your tone, Sorel; you seem to be taking things too much for granted. Perhaps you don't realize that I am making a great sacrifice! (*Pointing to Sandy*)

SOREL. Sorry, darling.

JUDITH (*starting to act*) It's far from easy, at my time of life, to——

SOREL (*playing up*) Mother—Mother, say you understand and forgive!

JUDITH. Understand! You forget, dear, I am a woman.

SORREL. I know you are, Mother. That's what makes it all so poignant.

JUDITH (*magnanimously, to Sandy*) If you want Sorel, truly, I give her to you—unconditionally.

SANDY (*dazed*) Thanks—awfully, Mrs Bliss.

JUDITH. You can still call me Judith, can't you?—it's not much to ask.

SANDY. Judith!

JUDITH (*bravely*) There, now. Away with melancholy. This is all tremendously exciting, and we must all be very happy.

SOREL. Don't tell Father—yet.

JUDITH. We won't tell anybody; it shall be *our* little secret.

SOREL. You are splendid, Mother!

JUDITH. Nonsense! I just believe in being honest with myself —it's awfully good for one, you know, so cleansing. I'm going upstairs now to have a little aspirin—— (*She goes upstairs, and turns*) Ah, Youth, Youth, what a strange, mad muddle you make of things!

(JUDITH *goes off upstairs.* SOREL *heaves a slight sigh*)

SOREL. Well, that's that!

SANDY. Yes. (*He sits on the form below the piano, looking very gloomy*)

SOREL. It's all right. Don't look so gloomy—I know you don't love me really.

SANDY (*startled*) I say, Sorel——

SOREL. Don't protest; you know you don't—any more than I love you.

SANDY. But you told Judith——

SOREL (*nonchalantly*) I was only playing up—one always plays up to Mother in this house; it's a sort of unwritten law.

SANDY. Didn't she mean all she said?

SOREL. No, not really; we none of us ever mean *anything*.

SANDY. She seemed awfully upset.

SOREL. It must have been a slight shock for her to discover us clasped tightly in each other's arms.

SANDY (*rising and moving to* c) I believe I do love you, Sorel.

SOREL. A month ago I should have let you go on believing that, but now I can't—I'm bent on improving myself.

SANDY. I don't understand.

SOREL. Never mind—it doesn't matter. You just fell a victim to the atmosphere, that's all. There we were alone in the library, with the windows wide open, and probably a nightingale somewhere about——

SANDY. I only heard a cuckoo.

SOREL. Even a cuckoo has charm, in moderation. (*She rises and goes to him*) You kissed me because you were awfully nice and I was awfully nice and we both liked kissing very much. It was inevitable. Then Mother found us and got dramatic—her sense of the theatre is always fatal. She knows we shan't marry, the same as you and I do. You're under absolutely no obligation to me at all.

SANDY. I wish I understood you a bit better.

SOREL. Never mind about understanding me—let's go back into the library.

SANDY. All right.

(*They go off through the door down* L. *After a moment's pause,* DAVID *and* MYRA *enter from the garden*)

DAVID. . . . and, you see, he comes in and finds her there waiting for him.

(*They come down* c)

MYRA. She hadn't been away at all?

DAVID. No; and that's psychologically right. I'm sure. No woman, under those circumstances, *would*.

MYRA (*sitting on the* L *end of the sofa*) It's brilliant of you to see that. I do think the whole thing sounds most excellent.

DAVID. I got badly stuck in the middle of the book, when the boy comes down from Oxford—but it worked out all right eventually.

MYRA. When shall I be able to read it?

DAVID. I'll send you the proofs—you can help me correct them.

MYRA. How divine! I shall feel most important.

DAVID. Would you like a cigarette, or anything?

MYRA. No, thank you.

DAVID. I think I'll have a drink. (*He goes to the table up by the window, and pours out some plain soda-water*)

MYRA. Very well; give me some plain soda-water, then.

DAVID. There isn't any ice—d'you mind?

MYRA. Not a bit.

DAVID (*bringing her drink*) Here you are. (*He goes back and pours himself a whisky-and-soda, and returns to the sofa*)

MYRA. Thank you. (*She sips it*) I wonder where everybody is.

DAVID. Not here, thank God.

MYRA. It must be dreadfully worrying for you, having a houseful of people.

DAVID (*sitting down by her side*) It depends on the people.

MYRA. I have a slight confession to make.

DAVID. Confession?

MYRA. Yes. Do you know why I came down here?

DAVID. Not in the least. I suppose one of us asked you, didn't they?

MYRA. Oh, yes, they asked me, but——

DAVID. Well?

MYRA. I was invited once before—last September.

DAVID. I was in America then.

MYRA. Exactly.

DAVID. How do you mean "exactly"?

MYRA. I didn't come. I'm a very determined woman, you know, and I made up my mind to meet you ages ago.

DAVID. That was charming of you. I'm not much to meet really.

MYRA. You see, I'd read *Broken Reeds*.

DAVID. Did you like it?

MYRA. Like it! I think it's one of the finest novels I've ever read.

DAVID. There now!

MYRA. How do you manage to know so much about women?

DAVID. I'm afraid my knowledge of them is sadly superficial.

MYRA. Oh, no; you can't call Evelyn's character superficial —it's amazing.

DAVID. Why are you being so nice to me? Have you got a plan about something?

MYRA (*laughing*) How suspicious you are!

DAVID. I can't help it—you're very attractive, and I'm always suspicious of attractive people, on principle

MYRA. Not a very good principle.

DAVID (*leaning towards her*) I'll tell you something—strictly between outrselves.

MYRA. Do!

DAVID. You're wrong about me.

MYRA. Wrong? In what way?

DAVID. I write very bad novels.

MYRA. Don't be so ridiculous!

DAVID. And you *know* I do, because you're an intelligent person.

MYRA. I don't know anything of the sort.

DAVID. Tell me why you're being nice to me.

MYRA. Because I want to be.

DAVID. Why?

MYRA. You're a very clever and amusing man.

DAVID. Splendid!

MYRA. And I think I've rather lost my heart to you.

DAVID. Shall we elope?

MYRA. David!

DAVID. There now, you've called me David!!

MYRA. Do you mind?

DAVID. Not at all.

MYRA. I'm not sure that you're being very kind.

DAVID. What makes you think that?

MYRA. You being rather the cynical author laughing up his sleeve at a gushing admirer.

DAVID. I think you're a very interesting woman, and extremely nice-looking.

MYRA. Do you?

DAVID. Yes. Would you like me to make love to you?

MYRA (*rising*) Really—I wish you wouldn't say things like that.

DAVID. I've knocked you off your plate—I'll look away for a minute while you climb on to it again. (*He does so*)

MYRA (*laughing affectedly. She puts her glass down on the table*) This is wonderful! (*She sits down again*)

DAVID (*turning*) That's right. Now then——

MYRA. Now then, what?

DAVID (*leaning very close to her*) You're adorable—you're magnificent—you're tawny——

MYRA. I'm not tawny.

DAVID. Don't argue.

MYRA. This is sheer affectation.

DAVID. Affectation's very nice.

MYRA. No, it isn't—it's odious.

DAVID. You mustn't get cross.

MYRA. I'm not in the least cross.

DAVID. Yes, you are—but you're very alluring

MYRA (*perking up*) Alluring?

DAVID. Terribly.

MYRA. I can hear your brain clicking—it's very funny.

DAVID. That was rather rude.

MYRA. You've been consistently rude to me for hours.

DAVID. Never mind.

MYRA. Why have you?

DAVID. I'm always rude to people I like.

MYRA. Do you like me?

DAVID. Enormously.

MYRA. How sweet of you!

DAVID. But I don't like your methods.

MYRA. Methods? What methods?

DAVID. You're far too pleasant to occupy yourself with the commonplace.

MYRA. And you spoil yourself by trying to be clever.

DAVID. Thank you.

MYRA. Anyhow, I don't know what you mean by commonplace.

DAVID. You mean you want me to explain?

MYRA. Not at all.

DAVID. Very well; I will.

MYRA. I shan't listen. (*She stops up her ears*)

DAVID. You'll pretend not to, but you'll hear every word really.

MYRA (*sarcastically*) You're so inscrutable and quizzical—just what a feminine psychologist should be.

DAVID. Yes, aren't I?

MYRA. You frighten me dreadfully.

DAVID. Darling!

MYRA. Don't call me darling.

DAVID. That's unreasonable. You've been trying to make me -all the evening.

MYRA. Your conceit is outrageous!

DAVID. It's not conceit at all. You've been firmly buttering me up because you want a nice little intrigue.

MYRA (*rising*) How dare you!

DAVID (*pulling her down again*) It's true, it's true. If it weren't, you wouldn't be so angry.

MYRA. I think you're insufferable!

DAVID (*taking her hand*) Myra—dear Myra——

MYRA (*snatching it away—she rises*) Don't touch me!

DAVID. Let's have that nice little intrigue. (*He rises*) The only reason I've been so annoying is that I love to see things as they are first, and then pretend they're what they're not.

MYRA. Words. (*She moves over* R) Masses and masses of words!

DAVID (*following her*) They're great fun to play with.

MYRA. I'm glad you think so. Personally, they bore me stiff.

DAVID (*catching her right hand again*) Myra—don't be statuesque.

MYRA. Let go my hand!

DAVID. You're charming.

MYRA (*furiously*) Let go my hand!

DAVID. I won't!

MYRA. You will!

(MYRA *slaps his face hard, and he seizes her in his arms and kisses her*)

DAVID (*between kisses*) You're—perfectly—sweet.

MYRA (*giving in*) David!

DAVID. You must say it's an entrancing amusement. (*He kisses her again*)

(JUDITH *appears at the top of the stairs and sees them. They break away, he still keeping hold of her hand*)

JUDITH (*coming down* c) Forgive me for interrupting.

DAVID. Are there any chocolates in the house?

JUDITH. No, David.

DAVID. I should like a chocolate more than anything in the world, at the moment.

JUDITH. This is a very unpleasant situation, David.

DAVID (*agreeably*) Horrible!

JUDITH. We'd better talk it all over.

MYRA (*making a movement*) I shall do nothing of the sort!

JUDITH. Please—please don't be difficult.

DAVID. I apologize, Judith.

JUDITH. Don't apologize—I quite understand.

MYRA. Please let go of my hand, David; I should like to go to bed. (*She pulls her hand away*)

JUDITH. I should stay if I were you—it would be more dignified.

DAVID (*moving a step towards Judith*) There isn't any real necessity for a scene.

JUDITH. I don't want a scene. I just want to straighten things out.

DAVID. Very well—go ahead.

JUDITH. June has always been an unlucky month for me.

MYRA. Look here, Judith—I'd like to explain one thing——

JUDITH (*austerely*) I don't wish to hear any explanations or excuses—they're so cheapening. This was bound to happen sooner or later—it always does, to everybody. The only thing is to keep calm.

DAVID. I am—perfectly.

JUDITH (*sharply*) There is such a thing as being too calm.

DAVID. Sorry, dear.

JUDITH. Life has dealt me another blow, but I don't mind.

DAVID. What did you say?

JUDITH (*crossly*) I said Life had dealt me another blow, but I didn't mind.

DAVID. Rubbish!

JUDITH (*gently*) You're probably irritable, dear, because you're in the wrong. It's quite usual.

DAVID. Now, Judith——

JUDITH. Ssshhh! Let me speak—it is my right.

MYRA. I don't see why.

JUDITH (*surprised*) I am the injured party, am I not?

MYRA. Injured?

JUDITH (*firmly*) Yes, extremely injured.

DAVID (*contemptuously*) Injured!

JUDITH. Your attitude, David, is nothing short of deplorable.

DAVID. It's all nonsense—sheer, unbridled nonsense!

JUDITH. No, David, you can't evade the real issues as calmly as that. I've known for a long time—I've realized subconsciously for years that you've stopped caring for me in "that way".

DAVID (*irritably*) What do you mean—"that way"?

JUDITH (*with a wave of the hand*) Just that way . . . It's rather tragic, but quite inevitable. I'm growing old now—men don't grow old like women, as you'll find to your cost, Myra, in a year or two. David has retained his youth astonishingly, perhaps because he has had fewer responsibilities and cares than I——

MYRA. This is all ridiculous hysteria.

DAVID (*going to Myra*) No, Myra—Judith is right. What are we to do?

MYRA (*furiously*) Do? Nothing!

JUDITH (*ignoring her*) Do you love her truly, David?

DAVID (*looking Myra up and down as if to make sure*) Madly!

MYRA (*astounded*) David!

DAVID (*intensely*) You thought just now that I was joking. Couldn't you see that all my flippancy was only a mask, hiding my real emotions—crushing them down desperately——?

MYRA (*scared*) But, David, I——

JUDITH. I knew it! The time has come for the dividing of the ways.

MYRA. What on earth do you mean?

JUDITH. I mean that I am not the sort of woman to hold a man against his will.

MYRA. You're both making a mountain out of a molehill. David doesn't love me madly, and I don't love him. It's——

JUDITH. Ssshhh!—you *do* love him. I can see it in your eyes—in your every gesture. David, I give you to her—freely and without rancour. We must all be good friends, always.

DAVID. Judith, do you mean this?

JUDITH (*with a melting look*) You know I do.

DAVID. How can we ever repay you?

JUDITH. Just by being happy. (*She sits on the sofa*) I may leave this house later on—I have a feeling that its associations may become painful, specially in the autumn——

MYRA. Look here, Judith——

JUDITH (*shouting her down*) October is such a mournful month in England. I think I shall probably go abroad—perhaps a *pension* somewhere in Italy, with cypresses in the garden. I've always loved cypresses, they are such sad, weary trees.

DAVID (*going to her, speaking in a broken voice*) What about the children?

JUDITH. We must share them, dear.

DAVID. I'll pay you exactly half the royalties I receive from everything, Judith.

JUDITH (*bowing her head*) That's very generous of you.

DAVID. You have behaved magnificently. This is a crisis in our lives, and thanks to you——

MYRA (*almost shrieking—moves over to Judith, but is stopped by David*) Judith—I *will* speak—I——

DAVID (*speaking in a very dramatic voice*) Ssshhh, Myra darling —we owe it to Judith to keep control of our emotions—a scene would be agonizing for her now. She has been brave and absolutely splendid throughout. Let's not make things harder for her than we can help. Come, we'll go out into the garden.

MYRA. I will *not* go out into the garden.

JUDITH (*twisting her handkerchief*) Please go. (*She rises to* LC) I don't think I can bear any more just now.

DAVID. So this is the end, Judith?

JUDITH. Yes, my dear—the end.

(*They shake hands sadly.* SIMON *enters violently from the garden and breaks in between them*)

SIMON. Mother—Mother, I've got something important to tell you.

JUDITH (*smiling bravely*) Very well, dear.

SIMON. Where's Sorel?

JUDITH. In the library, I'm afraid.

SIMON (*running to the library door and shouting off*) Sorel, come out—I've got something vital to tell you. (*He returns to* C)

DAVID (*fatherly*) You seem excited, my boy! What has happened?

(SOREL *enters with* SANDY *and remains down* L)

SOREL. What's the matter?

SIMON. I wish you wouldn't all look so depressed—it's good news!

DAVID. Good news! I thought perhaps Jackie had been drowned——

SIMON. No, Jackie hasn't been drowned—she's been something else.

JUDITH. Simon, what *do* you mean?

SIMON (*running up* C, *calling off*) Jackie—Jackie!

(JACKIE *enters coyly from the garden.* SIMON *takes her hand and leads her down* C)

She has become engaged—to me!

JUDITH (*in heartfelt tones*) Simon!

SOREL. Good heavens!

JUDITH. Simon, my dear! Oh, this is too much! (*She cries a little*)

SIMON. What on earth are you crying about, Mother?

Judith (*picturesquely*) All my chicks leaving the nest! Now I shall only have my memories left. Jackie, come and kiss me.

(Jackie *goes to her.* Simon *goes to* David, *who congratulates him*)

You must promise to make my son happy——
Jackie (*worried*) But, Mrs Bliss——
Judith. Ssshhh! I understand. I have not been a mother for nothing.
Jackie (*wildly*) But it's not true—we don't——
Judith. You're trying to spare my feelings—I know——
Myra (*furiously*) Well, I'm not going to spare your feelings, or anyone else's. You're the most infuriating set of hypocrites I've ever seen. This house is a complete feather-bed of false emotions —you're posing, self-centred egotists, and I'm sick to death of you.
Simon. Myra!
Myra. Don't speak to me—I've been working up for this, only every time I opened my mouth I've been mowed down by theatrical effects. You haven't got one sincere or genuine feeling among the lot of you—you're artificial to the point of lunacy. It's a great pity you ever left the stage, Judith—it's your rightful home. You can rant and roar there as much as ever you like——
Judith. Rant and roar! May God forgive you!
Myra. And let me tell you this——
Simon (*interrupting*) I'm not going to allow you to say another word to Mother——

(*They all try to shout each other down*)

Sorel		You ought to be ashamed of yourself——
Myra	(*together*)	Let me speak—I will speak——
David		Look here, Myra——
Judith		This is appalling—appalling!
Sorel		You must be stark, staring mad——
Myra		Never again—never as long as I live——
David	(*together*)	You don't seem to grasp one thing that——
Simon		Why are you behaving like this, anyhow?

(*In the middle of the pandemonium of everyone talking at once,* Richard *comes in from the garden. He looks extremely apprehensive, imagining that the noise is the outcome of Judith's hysterical confession of their lukewarm passion. He goes to Judith's side, summoning all his diplomatic forces. As he speaks everyone stops talking*)

Richard (*with forced calm*) What's happened? Is this a game?

(Judith's *face gives a slight twitch; then, with a meaning look at* Sorel *and* Simon, *she answers him*)

Judith (*with spirit*) Yes, and a game that must be played to the finish! (*She flings back her arm and knocks Richard up stage*)

SIMON (*grasping the situation*) Zara! What does this mean? (*Advancing to her*)

JUDITH (*in bell-like tones*) So many illusions shattered—so many dreams trodden in the dust——

DAVID (*collapsing on to the form in hysterics*) *Love's Whirlwind!* Dear old *Love's Whirlwind!*

SOREL (*running over to* R, *pushing Myra up stage and posing*) I don't understand. You and Victor—my God!

JUDITH (*moving away* L, *listening*) Hush! Isn't that little Pam crying——?

SIMON (*savagely*) She'll cry more, poor mite, when she realizes her mother is a—a——

JUDITH (*shrieking and turning to Simon*) Don't say it. Don't say it!

SOREL. Spare her that.

JUDITH. I've given you all that makes life worth living—my youth, my womanhood, and now my child. Would you tear the very heart out of me? I tell you, it's infamous that men like you should be allowed to pollute Society. You have ruined my life. I have nothing left—nothing! God in heaven, where am I to turn for help? . . .

SOREL (*through clenched teeth—swinging* SIMON *round*) Is this true? Answer me—is this true?

JUDITH (*wailing*) Yes, yes!

SOREL (*as if to strike Simon*) You cur!!!

JUDITH. Don't strike! He is your father!!!!

(JUDITH *totters and falls in a dead faint.* MYRA, JACKIE, RICHARD *and* SANDY *look on, dazed and aghast*)

CURTAIN

ACT III

SCENE—*The same. It is Sunday morning, about 10 o'clock.*
There are various breakfast dishes on a side table L, *and a big table is laid down* LC.

When the CURTAIN *rises* SANDY *appears at the top of the stairs. On seeing no-one about, he comes down furtively and quickly helps himself to eggs and bacon and coffee, and seats himself at the table. He eats very hurriedly, casting occasional glances over his shoulder. A door bangs somewhere upstairs, which terrifies him; he chokes violently. When he has recovered he tears a bit of toast from a rack, butters it and marmalades it, and crams it into his mouth. Then, hearing somebody approaching, he darts into the library.* JACKIE *comes downstairs timorously; her expression is dismal, to say the least of it. She looks miserably out of the window at the pouring rain, then assuming an air of spurious bravado, she helps herself to some breakfast and sits down and looks at it. After one or two attempts to eat it, she bursts into tears.* SANDY *opens the library door a crack, and peeps out.* JACKIE, *seeing the door move, screams.* SANDY *re-enters.*

JACKIE. Oh, it's only you—you frightened me!
SANDY. What's the matter?
JACKIE (*sniffing*) Nothing.
SANDY. I say, don't cry. (*He sits down at the table, facing her*)
JACKIE. I'm not crying.
SANDY. You were—I heard you.
JACKIE. It's this house. It gets on my nerves.
SANDY. I don't wonder—after last night.
JACKIE. What were you doing in the library just now?
SANDY. Hiding.
JACKIE. Hiding?
SANDY. Yes; I didn't want to run up against any of the family.
JACKIE. I wish I'd never come. I had horrible nightmares with all those fearful dragons crawling across the walls.
SANDY. Dragons?
JACKIE. Yes; I'm in a Japanese room—everything in it's Japanese, even the bed.
SANDY. How awful!
JACKIE (*looking up at the stairs to see if anyone is coming*) I believe they're all mad, you know.
SANDY. The Blisses?
JACKIE. Yes—they must be.
SANDY. I've been thinking that too.
JACKIE. Do you suppose they know they're mad?

47

SANDY. No; people never do.

JACKIE. It was Mr Bliss asked me down and he hasn't paid any attention to me at all. I went into his study soon after I arrived yesterday, and he said, "Who the hell are you?"

SANDY. Didn't he remember?

JACKIE. He did afterwards; then he brought me down to tea and left me.

SANDY. Are you really engaged to Simon?

JACKIE (*bursting into tears again*) Oh no—I hope not!

SANDY. You were, last night.

JACKIE. So were you—to Sorel.

SANDY. Not properly. We talked it over.

JACKIE. I don't know what happened to me. I was in the garden with Simon, and he was being awfully sweet, and then he suddenly kissed me, and rushed into the house and said we were engaged—and that hateful Judith asked me to make him happy!

SANDY. That's exactly what happened to me and Sorel. Judith *gave* us to one another before we knew where we were.

JACKIE. How frightful!

SANDY. I like Sorel, though; she was jolly decent about it afterwards.

JACKIE. I think she's a cat.

SANDY. Why?

JACKIE. Look at the way she lost her temper over that beastly game.

SANDY. All the same, she's better than the others.

JACKIE. That wouldn't be very difficult.

SANDY (*hiccupping loudly*) Hic!

JACKIE. I beg your pardon?

SANDY (*abashed*) I say—I've got hiccups.

JACKIE. Hold your breath.

SANDY. It was because I bolted my breakfast. (*He holds his breath*)

JACKIE. Hold it as long as you can.

(JACKIE *counts aloud. There is a pause*)

SANDY (*letting his breath go with a gasp*) I can't any more—hic!

JACKIE (*rising and getting a sugar basin from the side table down* L) Eat a lump of sugar.

SANDY (*taking one*) I'm awfully sorry.

JACKIE. I don't mind—but it's a horrid feeling, isn't it?

SANDY. Horrid—hic!

JACKIE (*putting the sugar basin down in front of Sandy and sitting again; conversationally*) People have died from hiccups, you know.

SANDY (*gloomily*) Have they?

JACKIE. Yes. An aunt of mine once had them for three days without stopping.

SANDY. How beastly!

JACKIE (*with relish*) She had to have the doctor, and everything.

SANDY. I expect mine will *stop* soon.

JACKIE. I hope they will.

SANDY. Hic! Damn!

JACKIE. Drink some water the wrong way round.

SANDY. How do you mean—the wrong way round?

JACKIE (*rising*) The wrong side of the glass. I'll show you. (*She goes to the side table* L) There isn't any water.

SANDY (*rising and standing below the table*) Perhaps coffee would do as well.

JACKIE. I've never tried coffee, but it might. (*She picks up his cup and hands it to him*) There you are!

SANDY (*anxiously*) What do I do?

JACKIE. Tip it up and drink from the opposite side, sort of upside down.

SANDY (*trying*) I can't reach any——

JACKIE (*suddenly*) Look out—somebody's coming. Bring it into the library—quick . . .

SANDY. Bring the sugar.

(JACKIE *picks up the sugar basin and runs into the library, leaving* SANDY *to follow*)

I might need it again—hic! Oh, God!

(SANDY *goes off into the library hurriedly.* RICHARD *comes downstairs. He glances round a trifle anxiously, goes to the window, looks out at the rain and shivers, then pulling himself together, he goes boldly to the barometer and taps it. It falls off the wall and breaks; he picks it up quickly and places it on the piano. Then he helps himself to some breakfast, and sits down on the* C *chair* L *of the table.*

MYRA *appears on the stairs, very smart and bright*)

MYRA (*vivaciously*) Good morning.

RICHARD (*half rising*) Good morning.

MYRA. Are we the first down?

RICHARD. No, I don't think so.

MYRA (*looking out of the window*) Isn't this rain miserable?

RICHARD. Appalling! (*He starts to drink his coffee*)

MYRA. Where's the barometer? (*She crosses to the side table* L)

RICHARD (*at the mention of the barometer, he chokes*) On the piano.

MYRA. What a queer place for it to be?

RICHARD. I tapped it, and it fell down.

MYRA. Typical of this house. (*At the side table*) Are you having eggs and bacon, or haddock?

RICHARD. Haddock.

MYRA. I'll have haddock too. I simply couldn't strike out a line for myself this morning. (*She helps herself to haddock and coffee, and sits down opposite Richard*) Have you seen anybody?

RICHARD. No.

MYRA. Good. We might have a little peace.

RICHARD. Have you ever stayed here before?

MYRA. No, and I never will again.

RICHARD. I feel far from well this morning.

MYRA. I'm so sorry, but not entirely surprised.

RICHARD. You see, I had the boiler room.

MYRA. How terrible!

RICHARD. The window stuck, and I couldn't open it—I was nearly suffocated. The pipes made peculiar noises all night, as well.

MYRA (*looking round the table*) There isn't any sugar.

RICHARD. Oh—we'd better ring.

MYRA. I doubt if it will be the slightest use, but we'll try.

RICHARD (*rising and ringing the bell, above the door* L) Do the whole family have breakfast in bed?

MYRA. I neither know—nor care.

RICHARD (*returning to his seat*) They're strange people, aren't they?

MYRA. I think "strange" is putting it mildly.

(CLARA *enters. She comes to the top of the table*)

CLARA. What's the matter?

MYRA. There isn't any sugar.

CLARA. There is—I put it 'ere myself.

MYRA. Perhaps you'd find it for us, then?

CLARA (*searching*) That's very funny. I could 'ave sworn on me Bible oath I brought it in.

MYRA. Well, it obviously isn't here now.

CLARA. Someone's taken it—that's what it is.

RICHARD. It seems a queer thing to do.

MYRA. Do you think you could get us some more?

CLARA. Oh, yes, I'll fetch you some (*She looks suspiciously and shakes her finger at Richard*) But mark my words, there's been some 'anky-panky somewhere.

(CLARA *goes out.* RICHARD *looks after her*)

MYRA. Clara is really more at home in a dressing-room than a house.

RICHARD. Was she Judith's dresser?

MYRA. Of course. What other excuse could there possibly be for her?

RICHARD. She seems good-natured, but quaint.

MYRA. This haddock's disgusting.

RICHARD. It isn't very nice, is it?

(CLARA *enters with sugar. She plumps it down on the table*)

CLARA. There you are, dear!

MYRA. Thank you.

CLARA. It's a shame the weather's changed—you might 'ave ad such fun up the river.

(*There comes the sound of a crash from the library, and a scream*)

What's that? (*She crosses to the door and flings it open*) Come out! What are you doing?

(JACKIE *and* SANDY *enter, rather shamefaced*)

JACKIE. Good morning. I'm afraid we've broken a coffee-cup.

CLARA. Was there any coffee in it?

SANDY. Yes, a good deal.

CLARA (*rushing into the library*) Oh dear, all over the carpet!

SANDY. It was my fault. I'm most awfully sorry.

(JACKIE *moves up* L *above the table.* CLARA *reappears*)

CLARA. How did you come to do it?

JACKIE. Well, you see, he had the hiccups, and I was showing him how to drink upside down.

MYRA. How ridiculous!

CLARA. Well, thank 'eaven it wasn't one of the Crown Derbys.

(CLARA *goes out*)

SANDY. They've gone now, anyhow! (*She moves up to the window and looks out*)

JACKIE. It was the sudden shock, I expect.

SANDY (*observantly*) I say—it's raining!

MYRA. It's been raining for hours.

RICHARD. Mrs Arundel——

MYRA. Yes?

RICHARD. What are you going to do about—about today?

MYRA. Nothing, except go up to London by the first train possible.

RICHARD. Do you mind if I come too? I don't think I could face another day like yesterday.

JACKIE. Neither could I. (*She comes down to the chair below Richard and sits*)

SANDY (*coming eagerly to the top of the table and sitting*) Let's all go away—quietly!

RICHARD. Won't it seem a little rude if we *all* go?

MYRA. Yes, it will. (*To Sandy*) You and Miss Coryton must stay.

JACKIE. I don't see why.

SANDY. I don't think they'd mind *very* much.

MYRA. Yes, they would. You must let Mr Greatham and me get away first, anyhow. Ring for Clara. I want to find out about trains.

(SANDY *rings the bell and returns to his seat*)

RICHARD. I hope they won't all come down now.

MYRA. You needn't worry about that; they're sure to roll about in bed for hours—they're such a slovenly family.

RICHARD. Have you got much packing to do?

MYRA. No; I did most of it before I came down.

(CLARA *enters and comes to the top of the table*)

CLARA. What is it now?

MYRA. Can you tell me what trains there are up to London?

CLARA. When?

MYRA. This morning.

CLARA. Why?—you're not leaving, are you?

MYRA. Yes; Mr Greatham and I have to be up by lunch-time.

CLARA. Well, you've missed the ten-fifteen.

MYRA. Obviously.

CLARA. There isn't another till twelve-thirty.

RICHARD. Good heavens!

CLARA. And that's a slow one.

(CLARA *goes out*)

SANDY (*to Jackie*) Look here, I'll take you up in my car as soon as you like.

JACKIE. All right; lovely!

MYRA. Oh, you have got a car, haven't you?

SANDY. Yes.

MYRA. Will it hold all of us?

JACKIE. You said it would be rude for us all to go. Hadn't you and Mr Greatham better wait for the train?

MYRA. Certainly not.

RICHARD (*to Sandy*) If there is room, we should be very, very grateful.

SANDY. I think I can squeeze you in.

MYRA. Then that's settled.

JACKIE. When shall we start?

SANDY. As soon as you're ready. (*He rises*)

JACKIE. Mrs Arundel, what are you going to do about tipping Clara?

MYRA. I don't know. (*To Richard*) What do you think?

RICHARD. I've hardly seen her since I've been here.

JACKIE. Isn't there a housemaid or anything?

RICHARD. I don't think so.

SANDY. Is ten bob enough?

JACKIE. Each?

MYRA. Too much.

RICHARD. We'd better give her one pound ten between us.

MYRA. Very well, then. Will you do it, and we'll settle up in the car?

RICHARD. Must I?

MYRA. Yes. Ring for her.

RICHARD. You'd do it much better.

MYRA. Oh, no, I shouldn't. (*To Jackie*) Come on; we'll finish our packing. (*She rises and goes to the stairs*)

JACKIE. All right. (*She follows Myra*)

(*They begin to go upstairs*)

RICHARD (*rising and going to* C) Here—don't leave me.

SANDY (*crossing to the door* R) I'll just go and look at the car. Will you all be ready in ten minutes?

MYRA. Yes, ten minutes.

(MYRA *goes off with* JACKIE)

SANDY. Righto!

(SANDY *rushes out.* RICHARD *moves over to the bell as* CLARA *enters with a large tray*)

CLARA. 'Allo, where's everybody gone?

RICHARD (*sorting out thirty shillings from his note-case*) They've gone to get ready. We're leaving in Mr Tyrell's car.

CLARA. A bit sudden, isn't it?

RICHARD (*pressing the money into her hand*) This is from all of us, Clara. Thank you very much for all your trouble.

CLARA (*surprised*) Aren't you a dear, now! There wasn't any trouble.

RICHARD. There must have been a lot of extra work.

CLARA. One gets used to that 'ere.

RICHARD. Good morning, Clara.

CLARA. Good morning, hope you've been comfortable.

RICHARD. Com—— Oh, yes.

(RICHARD *goes upstairs.* CLARA *proceeds to clear away the dirty breakfast things, which she takes out singing "Tea for Two" in a very shrill voice. She returns with a fresh pot of coffee, and meets* JUDITH *coming downstairs*)

JUDITH (*going to the head of the table and sitting*) Good morning, Clara. Have the papers come?

CLARA. Yes—I'll fetch them.

(CLARA *goes out and re-enters with the papers, which she gives to* Judith)

JUDITH. Thank you. You've forgotten my orange-juice.

CLARA (*pouring out a cup of coffee for Judith*) No, I 'aven't, dear; it's just outside.

(CLARA *goes out again.* JUDITH *turns to the theatrical column of the* "Sunday Times". SOREL *comes downstairs and kisses her*)

SOREL. Good morning, darling.

JUDITH. Listen to this. (*She reads*) "We saw Judith Bliss in a box at the Haymarket on Tuesday, looking as lovely as ever." There now! I thought I looked hideous on Tuesday.

SOREL. You looked sweet. (*She goes to get herself some breakfast, and sits* L *of Judith*)

(CLARA *reappears, with a glass of orange-juice*)

CLARA. There you are, dear (*placing it in front of Judith*). Did you see that nice bit in the *Referee?*

JUDITH. No—the *Times.*

CLARA. The *Referee's* much better. (*She finds the place and hands it to Sorel*)

SOREL (*reading*) "I saw gay and colourful Judith Bliss at the Waifs and Strays Matinée last week. She was talking vivaciously to Producer Basil Dean. 'I' sooth,' said I, 'where ignorance is Bliss, 'tis folly to be wise.' "

JUDITH (*taking it from her*) Dear *Referee!* It's so unselfconscious.

CLARA. If you want any more coffee, ring for it.

(CLARA *goes out*)

SOREL. I wish I were sitting on a lovely South Sea Island, with masses of palm-trees and coconuts and turtles——

JUDITH. It would be divine, wouldn't it?

SOREL. I wonder where everybody is.

JUDITH (*still reading*) I wonder . . . Mary Saunders has got another failure.

SOREL. She must be used to it by now.

(SIMON *comes downstairs with a rush*)

SIMON (*kissing Judith*) Good morning, darling. Look! (*He shows her a newly-completed sketch*)

JUDITH. Simon! How lovely! When did you do it?

SIMON. This morning—I woke early.

SOREL. Let's see. (*She takes the sketch from Simon*)

SIMON (*looking over her shoulder*) I'm going to alter Helen's face; it's too pink.

SOREL (*laughing*) It's exactly like her. (*She puts it on the chair beside her*)

JUDITH (*patting his cheek*) What a clever son I have!

SIMON. Now then, Mother! (*He gets himself breakfast*)

JUDITH. It's too wonderful—when I think of you both in your perambulators . . . Oh dear, it makes me cry! (*She sniffs*)

SOREL. I don't believe you ever saw us in our perambulators.

JUDITH. I don't believe I did.

(SIMON, *having got his breakfast, sits at the table* R *of Judith.* DAVID *comes downstairs*)

DAVID (*hilariously*) It's finished!
JUDITH. What, dear?
DAVID. *The Sinful Woman.* (*He kisses Judith*)
JUDITH. How splendid! Read it to us now.
DAVID (*taking a chair from the table and sitting* LC) I've got the last chapter here.
JUDITH. Go on, then.

(SANDY *rushes in from the front door. On seeing everyone, he halts*)

SANDY. Good morning.

(SANDY *bolts upstairs, two at a time. There is a pause; they all look after him*)

JUDITH. I seem to know that boy's face.
DAVID (*preparing to read*) Listen! You remember that bit when Violet was taken ill in Paris?
JUDITH. Yes, dear.—Marmalade, Simon.

(SIMON *passes it to her*)

DAVID. Well, I'll go on from there.
JUDITH. Do, dear.
DAVID (*reading*) "Paris in spring, with the Champs Élysées alive and dancing in the sunlight; lightly-dressed children like gay painted butterflies——"
SIMON (*shouting to Sorel*) What's happened to the barometer?
SOREL (*sibilantly*) I don't know.
DAVID. Damn the barometer!
JUDITH. Don't get cross, dear.
DAVID. Why can't you keep quiet, Simon, or go away.
SIMON. Sorry, Father.
DAVID. Well, don't interrupt again . . . (*Reading*) ". . . gay painted butterflies; the streets were thronged with hurrying vehicles, the thin peek-peek of taxi-hooters——"
SOREL. I love "peek-peek".
DAVID (*ignoring her*) "——seemed to merge in with the other vivid noises, weaving a vast pattern of sound which was Paris——"
JUDITH. What was Paris, dear?
DAVID. *Which* was Paris.
JUDITH. What was Paris?
DAVID. You can't say a vast pattern of sound *what* was Paris.

(*There is a slight pause*)

JUDITH. Yes, but—— What was Paris?
DAVID. A vast pattern of sound *which was Paris.*
JUDITH. Oh, I see.
DAVID. "Jane Sefton, in her scarlet Hispano, swept out of the Rue St Honoré into the Place de la Concorde——"
JUDITH. She couldn't have.

David. Why?

Judith. The Rue St Honoré doesn't lead into the Place de la Concorde.

David. Yes, it does.

Sorel. You're thinking of the Rue Boissy d'Anglas, Father.

David. I'm not thinking of anything of the sort.

Judith. David darling, don't be obstinate.

David (*hotly*) Do you think I don't know Paris as well as you do?

Simon. Never mind. Father's probably right.

Sorel. He isn't right—he's wrong!

David. Go on with your food, Sorel.

Judith. Don't be testy, David; it's a sign of age.

David (*firmly*) "Jane Sefton, in her scarlet Hispano, swept out of the Rue St Honoré into the Place de la Concorde——"

Judith. That sounds absolutely ridiculous! Why don't you alter it?

David. It isn't ridiculous; it's perfectly right.

Judith. Very well, then; get a map, and I'll show you.

Simon. We haven't got a map.

David (*putting his manuscript down*) Now, look here, Judith—here's the Rue Royale—(*he arranges the butter-dish and marmalade pot*) here's the Crillon Hotel, and *here's* the Rue St Honoré——

Judith. It isn't—it's the Boissy d'Anglas.

David. That runs parallel with the Rue de Rivoli.

Judith. You've got it all muddled.

David (*loudly, banging the table with his fist*) I have *not* got it all muddled.

Judith. Don't shout. You have.

Simon. Why not let Father get on with it?

Judith. It's so silly to get cross at criticism—it indicates a small mind.

David. Small mind my foot!

Judith. That was very rude. I shall go to my room in a minute.

David. I wish you would.

Judith (*outraged*) David!

Sorel. Look here, Father, Mother's right. (*She starts to draw a map*) Here's the Place de la Concorde——

Simon (*shouting at her*) Oh, shut up, Sorel!

Sorel (*shouting back at him*) Shut up yourself, you pompous little beast!

Simon. You think you know such a lot about everything, and you're as ignorant as a frog.

Sorel. Why a *frog*?

Judith. I give you my solemn promise, David, that you're wrong.

David. I don't want your solemn promise, because I *know* I'm right.

SIMON. It's no use arguing with Father, Mother.

SOREL. Why isn't it any use arguing with Father?

SIMON. Because you're both so pig-headed!

DAVID. Are you content to sit here, Judith, and let your son insult me?

JUDITH. He's your son as well as mine.

DAVID. I begin to doubt it.

JUDITH (*bursting into tears of rage*) David!

SIMON (*consoling her*) Father, how can you!

DAVID (*throwing his manuscript on the floor*) I'll never attempt to read any of you anything again, as long as I live. You're not a bit interested in my work, and you don't give a damn whether I'm a success or a failure.

JUDITH. You're dead certain to be a failure if you cram your books with inaccuracies.

DAVID (*hammering the table with his fist*) *I am not inaccurate!*

JUDITH. Yes, (*rising*) you are; and you're foul-tempered and spoilt.

DAVID. Spoilt! I like that! Nobody here spoils me—you're the most insufferable family to live with——

JUDITH. Well, why in heaven's name don't you go and live somewhere else?

DAVID. There's gratitude!

JUDITH. Gratitude for what, I'd like to know?

SOREL. Mother, keep calm.

JUDITH. Calm! I'm furious.

DAVID. What have you got to be furious about? Everyone rushing round adoring you and saying how wonderful you are——

JUDITH. I am wonderful, heaven knows, to have stood you for all these years!

SOREL. Mother, do sit down and be quiet. (*She rises*)

SIMON (*rising and putting his arm round his mother*) How dare you speak to Mother like that!

(*During this scene,* MYRA, JACKIE, RICHARD *and* SANDY *creep downstairs, with their bags, unperceived by the family. They make for the front door*)

JUDITH (*wailing*) Oh, oh! To think that my daughter should turn against me!

DAVID. Don't be theatrical.

JUDITH. I'm not theatrical—I'm wounded to the heart.

DAVID. Rubbish—rubbish—rubbish!

JUDITH. Don't you say Rubbish to me!

DAVID. I *will* say Rubbish!

(*They all shout at each other as loud as possible*)

Sorel		Ssshhh, Father!
Simon		That's right! Be the dutiful daughter and
	(together)	encourage your father——
David		Listen to me, Judith——
Judith		Oh, this is dreadful—dreadful!

Sorel		The whole thing doesn't really matter in the least——
Simon	*(together)*	—to insult your mother——
David		The Place de la Concorde——
Judith		I never realized how small you were, David. You're tiny——

(*The universal pandemonium is suddenly broken by the front door slamming. There is dead silence for a moment, then the noise of a car is heard.* Sorel *runs and looks out of the window*)

Simon (*flopping in his chair again*) There now!

Sorel. They've all gone!

Judith (*sitting down*) How very rude!

David (*also sitting down*) People really do behave in the most extraordinary manner these days——

Judith. Come back and finish your breakfast, Sorel.

Sorel. All right. (*She sits down*)

(*There is a pause*)

Judith. Go on, David darling; I'm dying to hear the end——

David (*picking up his manuscript from the floor; reading*) "Jane Sefton, in her scarlet Hispano, swept out of the Rue St Honoré into the Place de la Concorde——"

Curtain

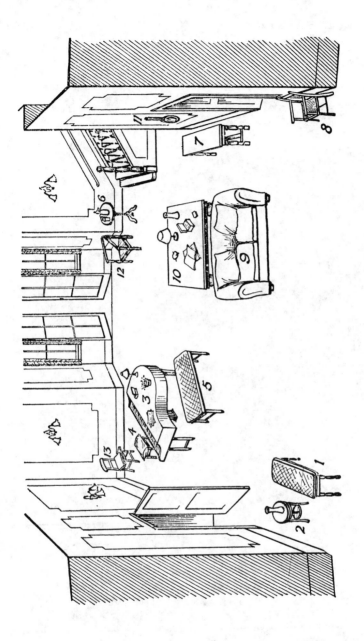

FURNITURE AND PROPERTY PLOT

ACT I

1. Stool (for 2 persons)
2. Small table. *On it:* vase (empty)
3. Baby grand piano. *On it:* cigarette-box, matches, ashtray, vase of sweet peas, mirror, pile of music, 2 magazines, table-lamp
4. Piano stool with cushion
5. Long stool
6. Table. (Soda siphon, decanter of whisky, 2 tumblers, vase of flowers)
7. Table
8. Armchair (rush-bottomed)
9. Sofa. *On it:* at rise, book of poems (for SOREL), 2 cushions
10. Closed dining-table. *On it:* ashtray, cigarette-box, matches, vase (empty), mirror, 2 books, table-lamp
11. Barometer, to fall in Act III and break
12. Three-cornered rush-bottomed armchair
13. Single rush-bottomed chair—with pile of music on it
    4 rugs down. 1 at C down stage
    1 at foot of stairs
    1 at C window
    1 at sofa down R

Pictures

On stage C—Cartridge paper, ruler, scissors, pencil (for SIMON)

Ready off down R—4 suitcases, 1 tennis-racket in case

Off up R—Gardening basket and flowers (for JUDITH)

Off up L—Small tea-tray. *On it:* teapot, sugar basin, cups and saucers, spoons, milk

Off up L—Tray with 8 cups and saucers, milk and sugar, plate of bread-and-butter, plate of cake (tea, milk, sugar—real)
    Teapot filled with tea
    Small stool to serve as tea-table (for CLARA)

Hand Props—Japanese cigarette-case (for RICHARD)

ACT II

Nothing extra on
Take tea-tray off
Take tea-stool off
Change vase of flowers on piano to 2 desk table and vase of sweet peas from this to piano.

ACT III

Take off—Sofa

Bring on—Dining-table and 7 chairs
    Dining-table laid for 7—7 side plates, 7 knives and forks, 7 fish knives and forks, marmalade in pot and spoon, 2 toast-racks with toast, condiments, butter in butter-dish
    Side plate at upper end of dining-table in centre of place

Butler's tray down L—8 cups and saucers and spoons, 1 jug of coffee, 1 jug of milk, sugar basin

On table half up L—8 plates, 2 covered dishes—(1) eggs and bacon for 3, (2) haddock for 5

Ready off up L—Serving table. *On it: Sunday Times* and *Referee* turned to theatrical column, 1 jug of coffee and jug of milk, glass with orange juice, common sugar basin with sugar, caricature for SIMON, MS. for DAVID (written)
            4 suitcases, racket in case

Ready off down L—"Door slam"
            "Cup break"

Ready off up R—Motor-car effect and motor-horn

Ready and working up C—Rain effect

MADE AND PRINTED IN GREAT BRITAIN BY
LATIMER TREND & COMPANY LTD PLYMOUTH

MADE IN ENGLAND